Murder Creek

OTHER BOOKS BY JOE FORMICHELLA

Schopenhauer's Maxim
Waffle House Rules
Scarpete Stories
The Wreck of the Twilight Limited
Whores for Life: Scatolo's, and other stories

NONFICTION

A Condition of Freedom
Staying Ahead of the Posse

MURDER CREEK: The Unfortunate Incident of Annie Jean Barnes

by Joe Formichella

with an introduction by Suzanne Hudson

Murder Creek

Copyright © 2007 by Joe Formichella. Introduction © 2007 by Suzanne Hudson. All rights reserved.

All rights reserved under International and Pan-American Copyright Conventions. Without limiting the rights under copyright reserved, no part of this publication may be reproduced, stored in or introduced into a retrieval system, or transmitted, in any form, or by any means (electronic, mechanical, photocopying, recording, or otherwise), without the prior written permission of both copyright owners. Waterhole Branch Productions, 2017.

Murder Creek

In memory of two women from opposite sides
of Murder Creek:

Annie Jean Barnes, East Brewton,
whose story is told in these pages

Catherine Caffey Gardner, Brewton,
who insisted that this story be told

Dedicated to those of Annie Jean's family who ask for,
and deserve, answers.

Murder Creek

Murder Creek

Introduction

SPEND A CHILDHOOD in any one place and that place sinks into you, for good or for ill, becoming a part of the intricate weave of your personality, your self. Images stamped on the retina day after day after day; warm repeated patterns of living, years of the hum of the same automobile engine, the rattle of familiar pot lids, the call of a mother at dusk; the camaraderie of playmates—all of this is absorbed by the spirit, taking it over at times, for good or for ill. The sense of loyalty and connectedness that comes with community is at the core of society. We need this. We construct it. We seek out a place where we can flourish. And, when that place is a small town, there is even more of an emotional investment—more of a connection, an "understood" level of interaction—that can be rich, supportive, and satisfying on the one hand but also duplicitous, or even conniving, on the other. All of this has been, at least, my own experience, having grown up in and, moreover, experienced, a small town.

Brewton, Alabama was an idyllic place to spend a childhood. Back in the homogeneous 1950s my street—Bonita Avenue, solidly middle to upper-middle class—was a reflection of the wholesome images that flickered at us from black and white Zenith television sets: the manicured lawns and happy homes of <u>Leave It To Beaver</u>, <u>Father Knows Best</u>, <u>The Donna Reed Show</u>; the knowledge that we were welcome in any of the houses on that street; the security of adult presences (a constant but at the periphery) while we were let loose to really, truly, play. We organized our own games, settled our own disputes, acted out imaginary scenarios for afternoons at a time, and roamed, expanding the borders of our world in increments without the neurotic, overly involved parents of today retarding our quest for independence. Our mothers—for it was the mothers who, along with the "help," were in our houses for the most part of the day—were happy to see us set out on summer mornings, the only rule being that we arrive back at dusk, since some mother or another in the neighborhood would certainly feed us peanut butter and jelly sandwiches with watered-down Kool-Aid at lunchtime.

As we grew older and into the early 1960s, we walked the few miles to the downtown area, passing the stately homes of the moneyed ones, to whom we gave little notice. We had more important things to do. We drank cherry cokes at the Moorman's Drugstore soda fountain, eyed the Villager and Bobbie Brooks dresses at The Fashion Shoppe, bought ninety-nine cent 45 rpm records at Robbins and McGowin Department Store, watched beach movies and sci-fi movies and Tarzan movies at the Ritz Theatre, oblivious to the overhead balcony filled with the black folks who worked in our kitchens, in our yards, and at the lumber mill that was the life's blood of the town. We walked to the Brewton Country Club, slathered on Coppertone in our two-piece bathing suits, cutting our eyes at Stephen Goodwin, the lifeguard, an older boy who would become an author and would write about things I was failing to see at the time. We would eat lunch in the pro shop, charging hamburgers and fries to our daddies, watching out the windows as the silent, square-topped golf carts glided across green perfection.

We rode our bicycles out to Kirkland, a sandy creek bank far into the woods, without any fear of being abducted by a pedophile or a rural rapist or a serial killer. The comfort zone of that place, Brewton and the country around it, was more than roomy enough, and the blend of my neighborhood and friendships was the depth of that comfort zone, one that I thought would last forever. But my sense of the place underwent a seismic shift, an awareness of the kind of glue necessary to keep together a certain façade, the recognition of injustice. It happened, almost to the day, on my thirteenth birthday.

The death of Annie Jean Barnes was an event that latched on to me because it laid bare the hypocrisy of my comfortable, TV family world. I was aware of rumors, of names mentioned, of housewives buzzing and wondering whose husbands had been at a camp house outside the city limits the weekend Annie Jean was found brutally beaten before dying in the hospital almost a week later. Some of the rumored names were prominent ones, either in the realm of social status or, more disturbing to me at the time, as pillars of the churches in town and as acquaintances of my family. It was a case that rent Brewton's beautiful veneer. It was a case that was whispered about feverishly, editorialized about with righteous indignation, and, even before the grand jury convened two months later, had already, for the most part, gone away in an intimidating rush. In the lingo of Orwell's 1984, "it was disappeared."

But it stayed with me.

A small community, I believe, does become a part of the weave of one's nature, and Brewton is a part of mine. But Annie Jean was not a Brewtonian; she lived in East Brewton, a separate municipality on the "wrong" side of Murder Creek, the side where the poor were much more populous than in Brewton proper, with its city school system, city parks, and fountained pools. Not that I was not oblivious to poverty; I had always been aware of the extreme "have-nots" in my school classes. Annie Jean Barnes' death made me aware, and much more important, fostered in me the potential for a depth of awareness I have come to over the years, and hopefully will continue to plumb, incrementally. She made me question the fabric of a place, of a community, of the individual parts of that community. Her death, or, in my opinion, her murder, forced me to notice the things Stephen Goodwin wrote about in his novel Kin, set in a fictionalized Brewton: the deep divisions of race, religion, class; divisions within families; divisions to ensure power—divisions that betray outward appearances.

Murder Creek

But are appearances so important? Do we focus so much on the superficial that we lose our ability to speak up for those who lack the power to be heard? My life on Bonita Avenue was idyllic; when I started really noticing things, at the age of thirteen, that "noticing" snowballed on through my formative years. I began to see more of my own weaknesses and the weaknesses of others. I wondered how it was, during the Civil Rights years, that so many folks who claimed to be Christians did not want black folks in their churches. I wondered how white mothers could entrust their babies to "colored women" and then refer to those women using racial epithets, a metallic tone of hatred in their voices. I wondered how people who enjoyed magnificent wealth—to the point of exorbitant, even pathetic excess—could see poverty or corruption just down the road, and still look at themselves in the mirror. I began to discover that my family had cracks in its own veneer, and, lo and behold, so did all of my friends' families. Whether it was booze or pills or philandering or mental illness, there was always bound to be a flaw hidden behind the finery and the fluff. Father didn't really Know Best and June Cleaver was a trick on white folks, just as, Flannery O'Connor once wrote, "Jesus is a trick on niggers." Smoke and mirrors, it seemed, were all over the place, and, unfortunately, the magicians still lurk.

"Why does Suzanne have to bring up that unfortunate incident?" I was told an elderly attorney wondered when my first novel, inspired by Annie Jean Barnes' death, came out. "Aren't you afraid?" other Brewtonians would ask, planting enough of a concern in me that I took to announcing at book events, "If I turn up dead, please investigate the Barnes case," followed by a little joke: "Or if I'm lucky they'll just wing me—hit an arm or a leg—and I can enjoy the surge in book sales." So, at the very worst, there are those who really do believe I should be afraid, suggesting that there might really be something dark and malevolent at play, some small cancer on the heart of the town. And, at the very least, there are many who truly want to leave the past in the past, where secrets are so safely tucked away and lives never have to be examined. I am sure that many will take this book as an assault on the good people and the good name of their town, objecting to a stain on the silk slipcover of Brewton, Alabama. Most of Annie Jean Barnes' children, however, would not be in that number, and that single fact, along with the fact that their questions have never been answered, have even been dismissed in a way that says, "Your mother doesn't matter; she is disposable," is enough to justify this book, in which Joe Formichella investigates the decades-old case. Murder Creek is a work of intriguing nonfiction, an account of his journey to find some answers for Annie Jean's son, Ralph, and Ralph's six siblings. Even more than that, it is multi-layered, exposing a larger system that was cynically designed to ensure that the Annie Jeans of Alabama would have no voice. It is about that tenacious underbelly of society that, while certainly not unique to Brewton, is all the more jarring because of the town's persona, wealth, and cosmetic appeal. It is also a story in which I became a reluctant character.

My initial resistance to partnering with Joe Formichella on this project goes back to my connection with the town, which, I will always maintain, was an idyllic place for a childhood, even, an effective place for a "coming of age." I feel that Brewton is a part of me just as I am still a part of it, in spite of the panic attacks that sometimes hit me when I see the city limits sign, when the reality of my self collides with the entrenched, inaccurate expectations of others. The familial friendships that are so much a part of my individual texture, which comes so much from growing up in Brewton, encompass a very wide circle, from intimate friends out to family friends, out to friends of friends, out to acquaintances—consistent ones, mere ones, and barely there ones. I did not want to offend anyone. But I had to decide, finally, it was okay for some—maybe even many—of those people to disapprove of, dislike, or even hate me, depending upon their emotional investment in the town's facade or in the case itself. In short, I had to ask myself if I were not, in my hesitancy to participate, a co-conspirator in the silence that has dragged at the soul of the town for years. Was I complacent enough to remain a guilty party without letting it affect my conscience, all because of what some might think of me? I did not want to drown in that depth of shallowness.

Murder Creek is, in its soul, meant to be an indictment—a permanent indictment—of those responsible for what happened to Annie Jean Barnes and what subsequently did not happen after her death. As a "throw-away" person from hardscrabble sharecropper roots, she was used, abused, and killed by those who were—whether they were actually present at the camp house or not—cogs in the machinery of wealth and power that kept Brewton's surface a shiny, squeaky clean. It is an indictment of law enforcement that, at the very least, sat on its hands. It is an indictment of codes of silence that protect the "good names" of men who do evil. It is an indictment of privilege and the twisted arrogance of the sense of entitlement that comes with it. Murder Creek is an indictment of those who could talk and answer key questions but who choose the kind of silence that has, throughout history, killed. It is an indictment of those who, even as they approach death, refuse to cave in to their consciences. Finally, it is an indictment of the truly good people of Brewton who perpetuate the secrecy, the hypocrisy, and the power structure by participating in it, giving it sustenance and energy, or simply by refusing to see it, giving it nourishment by default.

-- Suzanne Hudson

Fairhope, AL

Summer, 2007

Murder Creek

The Closing Argument

LADIES AND GENTLEMEN, this is a story of a poor young woman in south Alabama who was wholly dependent, economically, socially, physically, and emotionally, on the more privileged members of Brewton, and East Brewton, Alabama. Annie Jean Barnes—divorced, mother of seven children, loved by those children, as well as by their cousins, whose oldest child has said Annie Jean was as much a friend as a mother, a woman who trusted too much, perhaps, put too much faith in the goodness and guidance and well-meaning of others—was used, beaten, and then summarily disposed of by those who controlled her life, her resources, even her addiction, in September of 1966. This is what we know: We know that on the evening of Friday, September 16th, Ms. Barnes was summoned to the fishing camp of one, Dr. George Perry.

Picked up by Dr. Perry's personal assistant, she was brought to this place in the woods, a place, according to the lead investigator, where "a lot of shenanigans" went on, "drinking, partying, poker playing." We know that on the morning of September 18th, Annie Jean called her family for help. What they found was this once vibrant and playful woman brutally beaten, abused, and left to die on the kitchen floor of that camp. And there was no one else at the camp.

We know that upon her admission to the D.W. McMillan Hospital later that day, Annie Jean's attending physician reported that she was "suffering from multiple contusions and abrasions, badly swollen left arm and right breast." That she also had "multiple needle punctures and bruises on both arms" that there were "areas of her body that looked like they had been burned," and finally, that "she appeared to have been sexually assaulted." We know this same physician had reported that Annie Jean's condition improved during the week, that she was, quote, "feeling better." And finally we know that on Saturday morning, September 24th, mere hours after the first, the first, mind you, contact with state investigators looking into the case, Annie Jean suddenly died in that hospital. Here is the question before you, ladies and gentlemen, the mystery of our story: <u>Who beat Annie Jean Barnes</u>?

One week after she died, the Birmingham News, the leading newspaper in Alabama's largest city, in an article at the very top of page one, asked that very same question: "Who beat her?" A question, the reporter continued, "on the lips of just about every single one of the nearly 10,000 residents in this city." And yet, when local newspaper editors and radio talk show hosts asked the question "nearly every single" citizen wanted answered, they received death threats instead of answers. You have to ask yourself: What could be so sensitive about the answer to who beat this poor woman from the wrong side of Murder Creek that the lives of public commentators would be threatened for asking? Why, following a signed editorial on the 29th of September, would the editor of the Brewton Standard retreat from the condemnation of those responsible to all but silence in succeeding weeks? Power? Money? Prestige? Is that enough to silence good people from seeking the truth? Was that enough to sway the state's toxicologist to report that Annie Jean Barnes died of "natural causes," even though no one involved with the investigation has ever offered any explanation for exactly which "natural cause" led to her death? Is this the kind of community you want to live in?

I know what my answer is. My answer is no, no, not in Brewton, not in East Brewton; not in Alabama, not anywhere in these United States of America, do I want to live in a community where just because you might be rich, or powerful, you can cover up and dismiss the brutal beating and death of a young woman with seven young children, just because she's poor, just because she has nothing going for her but trust and faith in a system of justice designed to protect precisely those citizens too poor to wield any other kind of influence. The strength of a system of justice, the strength of a society, the strength of a community, any building, any structure, anything with any hopes of growing or prospering, is at the bottom, is measured by how we treat those on the bottom. A community that does not protect those at the bottom is not a very strong nor a very attractive community.

And yet we live in such a community. The editor of the Standard knows it. I know it. You know it. There are hundreds of such communities all across this land, where the entitled have the power and money, and the rest of us have little more than our faith. The case of Annie Jean Barnes is just another example of who wins the battle between power and faith, and who loses. That doesn't mean it isn't wrong. That doesn't mean it isn't outrageous. It is outrageous, I am outraged, as you should be outraged, that these men brought before you have the temerity and the gall to think they can control truth and justice only to benefit themselves, because it isn't just Annie Jean's, or her family's loss. We all lose. We lose our faith, and our community. And I do not think you want to continue to live in that kind of community. I know I don't, which is why, ladies and gentlemen, it will be up to you to finish this story, why you must, you must find the defendants guilty as charged.

*

Of course, that never happened. There was no trial. There were no defendants. There was no guilty verdict. What's more, there couldn't have been a trial. The Escambia County Grand Jury didn't see fit to return any indictments in the case of Annie Jean Barnes back in November of 1966, even though the salient facts alluded to and enumerated by our fictitious prosecutor are all true, or at least they are all part of the public record. State investigators never charged anyone. The central question of who beat Annie Jean Barnes was left unanswered, in large part because local law enforcement never bothered to ask. She probably would have told them, given that chance.

It remained unanswered some thirty-seven years, until September, 2003—the anniversary, coincidentally, of Annie Jean's hospital stay—with the publication of Suzanne Hudson's first novel, In A Temple of Trees. Then the question—along with many, many others—was finally asked once again.

The story of Annie Jean Barnes had no ending, was interrupted, cut off, and allowed to disappear, if only because the victim was viewed as disposable. Taking up the tale again has been a sorting out of fact and fiction, truth and rumor; a tale about the determined will of a story to be told, no matter how much power, money, influence, malfeasance, reluctance or time are brought to bear upon silencing that story. It is a story, additionally, about the best and the worst of the State of Alabama, and as such resonates with the best and the worst of the nation, because ultimately, it is a story about the rule of law, what's been called the single greatest achievement of this society, our principal, sometimes only defense (at least in theory) against both mob rule and over-reaching power. Mostly, it is the story of the "mysterious death of young divorcee" Annie Jean Barnes, to quote the banner headline of the October 1, 1966 edition of the Birmingham News, a woman whose biggest mistake may have been trusting too willingly that such notions as equal protection really and truly applied to everyone.

Annie Jean probably was guilty of trusting too soon, or too well. Most of her romantic encounters would bear that out, from the father of six of her children, Fred Barnes, to Dr. Perry himself. But because trust is built up over time, through continued experience, Annie Jean's transgression might better be considered a matter of faith, albeit faith unwisely placed and she seemed to know it. She told a friend from her hospital bed, hours before she died there, tears welling in her eyes at the mention of the responsible party, "You are just like me," adding, "You wouldn't believe it if I told you," wouldn't believe how quickly the story could turn, how awful it could become.

So where does such a story truly begin? That September Friday night in 1966, the last time her eldest son Ralph, child of an ill-conceived high school romance, would see her alive, as he was coming in the door, returning from a high school football game, and she was leaving? At the start of her illicit romance with Dr. Perry four years before that? With her birth, in the depths of the Great Depression, a catastrophe that hit Alabama extremely hard (as one historian has characterized it, for many Alabamians, like Annie Jean's family it meant only that tough, tough times, just got more difficult[1]) in 1934?

In the widest sense, if the theories of Bohr and Einstein can't adequately be reconciled—the great dilemma—it might be reasonable to ask where does any story begin? And yet, in this case it is possible to locate a seminal moment when the factors and the forces that would ultimately result in the unfolding of this "unfortunate incident" of Annie Jean Barnes are set in place. That moment was September 3, 1901, when the still-current Alabama State Constitution was completed—not when it was ratified, or signed into law, but when it was completed, because that was the moment the fate of Annie Jean and the rest of Alabama's poor was sealed—sixty-five years before. Quoting the September 29, 1966 edition of the Brewton Standard: "The peace and quiet of this small South Alabama city was abruptly shattered during the past week-end when a relatively unknown 31-year old woman died in circumstances that have fanned the flames of rumors, doubts and most of all sheer amazement that this could happen here."

What follows is the story, how we received it, how we pursued it, the whole story, or as much of the story as possible, without varnish, polish, or augmentation. It encompasses the facts, the fictions, the rumors, and, hopefully, finally, after forty years, the truth. But first:

Murder Creek

ACCORDING TO LOCAL legend, sometime in 1788, a British royalist was making his way from South Carolina to Pensacola, Florida, where he hoped to obtain passports and thus passage into the Spanish province of Louisiana. Colonel Kirkland and his party—a son, a nephew, and two other white men, as well as a native guide—encountered a pack-horse party traveling in the opposite direction, coming from a trading expedition in Pensacola. They were within a mile of a large creek that flowed into the Conecuh River, in what was then vastly unpopulated, forested territory of Georgia but today is Escambia County, Alabama. This other party consisted of, among others, a Hillabee Indian who had murdered so many men that he was called Istillicha, the man slayer; a fugitive white man, referred to by the Indians as Catt, because of his ferocity and viciousness, and the slave of a Creek Indian trader, called Bob. Shortly after their chance meeting, the latter party stopped, hatched a plot, and turned around. Kirkland and his group, meanwhile, crossed what was called Aloochahatcha Creek, and settled by the side of the trading path for the night, just south of present day Brewton. Reclining their muskets against a large live oak tree—with branches as stout as any pack mule and trailing whispery Spanish moss—and placing their saddle bags, loaded down with pieces of silver, under their heads, Kirkland and the rest soon fell asleep.

At midnight, Istillicha, Catt, and Bob quietly crossed the creek. Bob crept up to the big tree, seized Kirkland's idle gun, and "blowed his brains out."[2] Catt and Istillicha rushed in with hatchets and knives. Kirkland's son jumped up and pleaded for his life to be spared. Catt replied, "We did not come to hear talks,"[3] and slit his throat. They killed the rest of the party except for three servants, burned Kirkland's papers, and emptied the saddlebags of silver. The murderers then divided the loot amongst themselves, and proceeded to the Creek nation.

Alexander McGillivary, the Indian, French, and Scots Chief of the Creek Indians, had provided Kirkland with the native guide to insure his safe passage through the territory. When news of the ambush reached him he dispatched a group of men after the perpetrators. Though the others escaped, Catt was arrested, returned to the spot of the bloody attack and strung from the same tree where Kirkland's guns had been resting. The posse eventually put an end to his dangling and kicking with a pistol ball. Aloochahatcha has been known as Murder Creek ever since.[4]

Eighty years later, in December of 1868, at the height of Reconstruction, Escambia County was created. The name, according to The Heritage of Escambia County (2002), is Creek for either "clear water," or "place where you might gather cane." The original name for the land between Burnt Corn and Murder Creeks was Crossroads, and then Newport, after the Alabama and Florida railroad came through in the spring of 1861 and a new station was built there. Shortly afterward it was changed to Brewton, in honor of the first depot agent, Edmund Troupe Brewton,[5] and incorporated by an act of legislature February 13, 1885.

The first Escambia county seat was in Pollard, a few miles to the south of Brewton. Pollard is best known, perhaps, for a disdainful quip from Mark Twain. Stranded there for a time after a train wreck, he is supposed to have said he'd "rather die in vain than live in Pollard, Alabama."[6] The seat was moved to Brewton in June of 1883, after the Pollard courthouse burned, following the legendary "cat train" episode.*

---

* The story goes that the citizens of Brewton, which was growing faster and was much more prosperous than Pollard, conducted a strenuous and vocal lobbying

Those were, reportedly, heady years for Brewton: "During the 1880s there were five hotels and two boarding houses in use. Harold Brothers Commissary was built in 1878. It was the first brick building constructed in Brewton. Later, in 1894, a three-story building was constructed just north of the Harold Commissary and in 1896 became the Robbins and McGowin Store."[7] Some seventy years later, Annie Jean Barnes would work for a time as a secretary in the offices of Ed Leigh McMillan, located above what was then a clothing store in the Robbins and McGowin building.

East Brewton wasn't incorporated until 1918. But an area of the town, Fort Crawford, was the earliest settlement in the county, having been established in 1813 because of its strategic, elevated site on the eastern side of Murder Creek for the ease of monitoring the activities of the Spanish to the south, the Creeks to the west. And the Crawford Cemetery, nestled up to the bluff which overlooks the creek, is the final resting place for members of some of the most prominent families in Brewton, including Robbins, McGowin, Langham, and Sowell, who founded the Bank of Brewton.

In some places (San Antonio, even other places in Alabama, like Montgomery) a body of water coursing through town signifies possibility, potential, means and services and goods that will always be available, the pulse of the waterway insuring vitality, sustenance, a future. With the development of Brewton, and then East Brewton—not a sister city by any means; more like a

---

campaign for the seat. Pollard resisted. A reporter for the *Brewton Blade* observed that it all sounded like little more than a cat fight, to which Pollard is said to have responded, "if they want a cat fight, we'll give them a cat fight." They then loaded up a freight car with stray cats, trucked it north, and released them in downtown Brewton. (From *History of Escambia County*)

neglected step-child—Murder Creek signified something closer to the Rio Grande, after the military accession of Mexican territory in the Southwest, or, closer to home, the Mississippi that separates St. Louis from East St. Louis, than the Alabama or the San Antonio rivers: Murder Creek is a border, an obstacle, a dividing line between the haves and the never-going-to-gets, just like the Mississippi separating thriving St. Louis from the "urban prairie" of East St. Louis. "There was no access to Brewton from East Brewton," I've been told, "except for jocks," by someone who had first-hand experience, a jock in East Brewton, and then a teacher in Brewton, who went to high school with Annie Jean's younger brothers. The only thing that successfully straddled the creek between the two towns was the T. R. Miller Mill Company, built in 1892.

Timber, and then the oil beneath the tracks of privately owned forests accounted for the vast wealth of those "haves" in Brewton. But that wealth was shared and passed on amongst only a handful of families, earning the city the designation at one point as possessing the highest per-capita income of any city in the region. A 1925 Chamber of Commerce pamphlet, "Make Our Town Your Town," boasted, among other things, "one of the largest yellow pine lumber manufacturing plants in the south," with a payroll of nearly a million 1925 dollars, and additionally, that "the value of Brewton's church properties is more in proportion to population than in any other city in the South," the finest hotel between Mobile and Montgomery, a nine hole golf course, and no mosquitoes, all for a population, according to the 1924 census, of 3200. But while T. R. Miller, an illiterate man who struck it rich with his timber acquisitions in the late 1800s, could buy whatever prestige or position he wanted, and who started his own Universalist church after being shunned by the Methodists in town, George Perry's parents were poor tenant farmers in Southeast Alabama, and Annie Jean's family moved from logging site to logging site, her father a turpentine dipper, an awful, painstaking task that yielded very little reward for the effort, completely dependant upon the company.

The dipper was the lowest, least-skilled, least paid worker in the turpentine camps that worked the long-leaf pine forests from the Carolinas through Georgia, Alabama, and into the Florida panhandle. The foreman of the camp, who rode horseback throughout the day, overseeing his men, could earn $2.50 a day, according to recorded WPA expeditions into the camps in the 1930s. Under the foreman were the choppers, who made the slanting cuts in the trunks of the trees to induce sap flow; pullers, who were specialized choppers using a custom-made tool smithed in Connecticut, to reach higher portions of the trunks; and finally the dippers, who scraped the gum out of the cup with an iron. A dipper would earn 85 cents for a barrel of gum, with the best of them collecting no more than two barrels a day. Turpentining halted from November through March, when it was too cold for the sap to run. Many of the workers then became indigent migrants, moving their families to another potential site. And when there was work to be found in the camps, it was almost uniformly performed by blacks, as documented in the reports of Zora Neale Hurston at Cross City, Florida, and Helen S. Hartley of the camp at Padgett's Switch, Alabama, south of Mobile. An earlier history recorded by Frederick Law Olmsted said that in North Carolina, slaves were used in the turpentine camps because cotton was not as big a crop there as in other southern states.

Olmsted went on to say, "the Negroes employed in this branch of industry seem to me to be unusually intelligent and cheerful. Decidedly they are superior in every moral and intellectual respect to the great mass of the white people inhabiting the turpentine forest." Of the latter, he wrote, "there is a large number, I should think a majority, of entirely uneducated, poverty stricken vagabonds."[8]

Murder Creek

The Windhams, Annie Jean's maiden name, though white, occupied the lowest of post-reconstruction socio-economic orders, as did the Perrys, tenant farming being little more than the bastard child of plantation slavery. Which is exactly how the land owners, the timber barons, and the industry mules of Alabama wanted that era's society to be structured, for the protection and accumulation of their own wealth and power, their children's inheritance of those assets, and on into perpetuity.

Murder Creek

Brewton, Alabama

THAT BREWTON GREW and was finally incorporated in the decade succeeding Reconstruction is no small coincidence. Thom Hartmann cites the period as the first great, concentrated effort to destroy the American middle class, and thus, democracy itself. "The concepts of owning a home, having health or job security, and enjoying old age were unthinkable for all but the mercantile class and the rich. America seemed to be run for the robber barons and not for the thousands who worked for them. Democracy in America was at its lowest ebb; our nation more resembled the Victorian England that Dickens wrote of than the egalitarian and middle-class-driven democracy that Alexis de Tocqueville saw here in 1836," he writes, but then goes on to say, "That all changed in the 1930s,"[9] with FDR. And it was in the 30s when revisionist scholars started to peer through the "smokescreen" of equal rights and focus more on economic rather than political or constitutional issues as a means of understanding the machinations of Reconstruction. "[E]xpanding capitalism" was "the chief corrupting agent" of the period, T. Harry Williams wrote.[10] That corruption came to full flower in Alabama at the 1901 Constitutional Convention. And if the framers of that constitution had drawn a blueprint for an actual place in the world they imagined and preferred to live, a fabled, Oz-like city, where form and function exactly reflect attitude and belief, the result would have been Brewton.

"Welcome to Brewton," a free-standing theater marquee says, greeting automobile traffic on the south-west corner where highways 29 and 31 intersect, on the edge of downtown. The marquee is all that's left of the former Ritz movie theater which used to be on the site. Suzanne remembers the movie house as plush, with a wide foyer, velvet drapes, running lights down the aisles, and a balcony, where up until 1970 or so, black patrons sat.

From the gulf coast, the city is about an hour and a half drive north on highway 31, a four-laned blacktop separated by a wide grassy median through Loxley and Baldwin County's seat, Bay Minette, where it collapses down to two lanes, toward the Escambia County line.

The drive is, literally, a trip into the woods. Just across the county line a dead deer lies sprawled by the roadside, signifying the main attraction of the area. Hunters can be seen in pick-up trucks and on four-wheelers, dressed out in their camouflage and glaring orange vests and billed caps. The highway is lined with tall, long-leaf pine groves on both sides, rows of anemic looking trees all leaning as one with whatever direction the last big blow had come from. An occasional trunk is snapped halfway up and folded over on itself, like a nearly closed switchblade, the tuft of needles at what was the crown gone brown. No more than twenty-five, thirty feet of easement buffers the road, where power lines supported by concrete utility poles—less susceptible to hurricane force winds—carry electricity into the country. Threading through the overgrown pine and scrub oak thicket, a set of CSX railroad tracks parallels the road all the way northward. An occasional dirt path of rutted red clay trails off to the left or right, disappearing into the woods. Any structures fronting the road, on the side where the railroad runs, look like they've absorbed years of rumbling freight trains and blasts from the whistles, vibrations rattling joists and girders and rivets. There is an auto salvage yard, a sprawling fenced pen of picked over cars propped up on wheel rims, missing hoods and doors. Warehouse buildings have been raised here and there. Other than that, most dwellings outside of the small towns are trailers, whose insides—used up appliances, misplaced tools, and neglected toys—have spilled out onto the patchy lots.

Murder Creek

Empty and idle pulpwood trucks appear in the yards of the trailers as you get closer to the paper mills. In Flomaton a farm tractor rolling down the highway at about twenty miles an hour slows traffic before turning off into a field. On the outskirts of Brewton an old motel is now the home of itinerant pulp-wooders, whose trucks clog the parking lot.

At that main intersection in Brewton, by the Welcome to Brewton sign—"Voted one of the country's 100 best small towns"—a right turn onto 29 takes you across the Buddy Mitchell bridge over Murder Creek, into East Brewton, "A city of Vision, Growth, Progress." Highway designates 31 and 29 actually converge at Flomaton, and are one and the same for fourteen miles. Not so, once in Brewton.

The business district of East Brewton is situated on a one mile stretch of 29: a produce stand on the left, then a First Church of the Nazarene, across from a Community of Christ, next to a tax service, the First Methodists, a Gas-and-Gro, a Fred's—facing Horton's Plaza—a John Deere dealership, a lot of storage sheds that also houses Yvonne's Beauty Salon and Tanning, until a thrift store, and then an Assembly of God. And that's all. W. S. Neal High School sits a few blocks over, situated in the midst of a grid of homes ranging from modest to crumbling.

Turning north on Snowden Road, between the Church of the Nazarene and Horton's, a park is now located where a long row of shanties once stood. It was in this lost neighborhood where the Windham children grew up and the Barnes family lived until Annie Jean died. The shacks have all been torn down, but locals remember a cluster of squalid rough wooden buildings with leaning porches and dirt yards full of children, dogs, and abandoned cars. Farther up Snowden the homes crowded around the Fort Crawford Cemetery don't look much better.

The area is so poor, the lowest of low-class, that those residents wouldn't have been able to vote prior to 1966. East

Murder Creek

Brewton and Brewton, despite being divided by only the twenty-five feet of Murder Creek, are two distinct municipalities, with separate school systems and separate community services. East Brewton was mostly "white trash," blue collar folks who worked for the Rural Electric Authority or Harold's veneer mill, or across the creek at one of the big mills, T.R. Miller Mill Company or Container Corporation of America, or at Chem-Strand near Pensacola, Florida, rising well before dawn to catch a bus packed with other employees of the chemical manufacturer. The town contained very little mercantile presence, with Fountain's Grocery and Horton, the tax assessor. There were no rich in East Brewton, and no blacks except out on the very edge of town, along Ridge Road. The stretch of homes along Snowden, before the cemetery, was so neglected the city didn't even bother them about adhering to building, utility, or sanitation codes. Anyone who held a job there was most likely a day-laborer for the pulpwood truckers. (Yet after Annie Jean's death, Lovie Windham, along with the orphaned Barnes children, found the resources to move into a modern brick home farther out Snowden, beyond the church. Willie Mae Dawkins, too, found herself living in a new home, one much nicer than what she was accustomed to inhabiting.)

Back westward on 29, veering to the right for the bypass into Brewton, the road takes you into the heart of downtown, to the original brick Bank of Brewton building, the oldest bank in Alabama. North of downtown, down a side road past T. R. Miller Mill Company, most of Brewton's black population lives between the railroad tracks and the creek. Rows of shacks line the service road, but their lives are still better for being on the west side of the water. Legend has it that a nineteenth century outlaw, Railroad Bill, used to ride the rails between Atmore, Pollard, Flomaton, Brewton, and Evergreen, stealing freight and food from the railroads and dispensing it from the moving cars to the poor blacks who lived along the route. Railroad Bill was the Robin Hood of south Alabama, until he was ambushed and killed by Sheriff

McGowin in 1897, his body put on display in Montgomery, Brewton, and finally Pensacola, as a warning of what could happen if you flouted the law.

Brewton's black population has spilled over those railroad tracks, along Sowell Road, past the Baptist Hill Cemetery. The houses sit right on top of one another, as if the land had only grudgingly been granted. Run-down homes and abandoned buildings line the road. Kids stand in the street at intersections, watching the traffic their only entertainment. At the corner of Martin Luther King Jr. Street, the entire front of a house is collapsed, like some giant inadvertently stepped on it.

The former Booker T. Washington high school, now Brewton Middle School, sat closed for many years after integration finally came to Brewton's schools, a decade and a half after Brown v. Board of Education. If the city was going to abide by the Supreme Court edict, it wasn't going to be the white children who'd be relocated. There was no civil rights upheaval in Brewton, possibly because it was so strictly divided, and perhaps because an exclusive Dutch Reform-supported private boarding school, Southern Normal, siphoned off enough of the local black students to make them less of a presence in the public school in town. Longtime white residents, however, like to point to the lack of incident as evidence of their tolerance and as an example of how integration should be executed.

Mary Tucker, a former Normal student and then employee, who has since moved to Monroeville, (hometown of Truman Capote and Harper Lee, located an hour and a half to the west) remembers Brewton during the Civil Rights years a little bit differently. Tucker grew up in Conecuh, just north of Brewton, but moved there to attend Southern Normal. She went on to attend a Dutch Reform affiliated college in Iowa. She remembers petitioning the local newspaper to change its insidious policy of not using proper titles when referring to blacks in their articles, a policy employed by most Southern newspapers—just another not-so-subtle maneuver to subjugate. She remembers, too, a Dr. Langford heading up the local NAACP chapter, making himself a regular target of the newspaper. In one of her confrontations with the publisher, she invited him to the organization's meetings, but says he refused. Tucker makes a point of saying they were denied use of the public library and then scoffs at the all-too-typical attitude among whites concerning Jim Crow segregation, the ridiculous notion that "they" liked it that way.

"No we didn't," she says, not even bothering to disguise her scorn. "We just couldn't do anything about it," in a world where they were deemed not equal enough to deserve a respectful title, much less anything like full representation or equal protection.

Down Sowell Street, across Gordon, you enter what's still referred to as "white man's land." Here the homes are sturdy, brick, with kept lawns and sidewalks. Back across 31, past the ultra-modern T. R. Miller High School, "Home of the Tigers," and their huge football stadium, sit the truly elite sections of town. Brewton operates one of only two city-run school systems in the state. Brewton schools, though public, operate beyond the control and influence of the county system, and they don't have to share their portion of state funding. The only private school in Brewton was the aforementioned Southern Normal, which shut down toward the close of the millennium. The reason Brewton's gentry didn't simply open a private school, according to a former teacher in the system, is that there weren't enough privileged children to fill the classrooms, and they didn't want to appear too ostentatious. "Appearance is very important in Brewton," the sociology teacher said.

Riding along Belleville and Evergreen is a trip through the antebellum south. Stately, columned mansions sit far off the roadway, fronted by manicured lawns and ornate brickwork. The big, beautiful First Methodist Church has a twenty-foot stained-glass Jesus, welcoming arms wide open, inlaid in the masonry wall. McMillan Memorial Hospital has grown up around the original clinic buildings that had separate white and colored waiting rooms back in 1966. Farther south on Belleville is the public library, and the only home along that stretch in disrepair has a terminal white column out of joint, and a rain gutter dangling. Across the street is where a Brewton reading club met, in "King" David Miller's old home, a green clapboard and brick house with upstairs and downstairs verandas, nestled behind lush azalea bushes. One of the McMillan spreads, a sprawling white ranch house, had an indoor pool with a retractable roof. Past T. R's former Universalist Church, a granite castle, thick with climbing ivy, past the courthouse, is a place where the lawyers might lunch regularly, Old Willie's Restaurant, across from the Bank of Brewton complex. It was in Willie's one night in September of 2003 that the idea to pursue the story of Annie Jean was first hatched.

There are only three thoroughfares through Brewton: Highway 31, Belleville Avenue, and its parallel, Highway 29, what's called St. Nicholas Road on the Brewton side of the creek. St. Nicholas is where Brewton's poor whites live, flanking the west side of town. There is a park now on the corner of 31 and St. Nicholas, where the welcoming marquee stands, and a walking path winds through the open space. Just a little north of the intersection used to be slum apartments, the L & S Apartments, for Lovelace & Stokes, "where the poorest of the poor lived," Suzanne Hudson said, during a recent tour of the city, recalling a childhood visit to deliver a Brownie scout uniform to a girl who couldn't afford one. She had been shocked to see a newborn baby in its makeshift crib: a cardboard box on the kitchen table.

Farther up St. Nicholas are more dilapidated shacks, crowded together, competing for the same space and air. A turn off St. Nicholas onto one of the side streets, up near O'Bannon park, is a journey into a third world ghetto, mangy dogs with distended bellies snarling from under crumbling porches. The street dead-ends at the woods, and it is too narrow and cluttered to turn around without tracking across someone's dirt yard. You worry about who's watching the maneuver behind the darkened, naked windows. Suzanne points out where the city swimming pool was, on the south end of the park. It, too, was drained and closed after integration, rather than have whites and blacks swimming together. The white children of those who made such decisions could always swim in the country club's pool.

On the other side of the street the shacks have been torn down, demolished after recent hurricane damage, perhaps, and the lots cleared. "Rich folks expanding their backyards," Suzanne says. Looking up the sloping lots you can see the backs of some of the mansions, looming over the town. They can look out their back windows and see the squalor. And you wonder if it's always been like that.

"The only thing that's changed about Brewton," Suzanne answered, "is more Pizza Huts."

"Did you like growing up in Brewton?" I asked.

"Well, sure."

"Why?"

"The sense of security, safety. As kids, we could go out, disappear for a whole day, ride our bikes for miles to the creeks, come home at dusk, and nobody worried about us."

"What didn't you like about the town?"

"All the isms," she said.

I asked her father, Gene, the same set of questions. He said what he liked about Brewton was the close community. "We had some good, good friends," he said. "And there was a sense, too, that when Brewton decided to do something," a new school, the

YMCA, the country club, "they were going to do it first class," in large part because of the resources and support of the company.

"The company," he said, meaning the T.R. Miller Mill Company, "is the town."

Gene came to Brewton, and the company, in 1958, just after the paper mill had gone into production. Brewton had won the bid for the mill because T. R. Miller guaranteed them raw material. Between the two they are the life's blood, and largest benefactors of Brewton. When the black community needed access to their cemetery, a T. R. Miller road crew went out and built it, on company time. When the city needed a forklift to move waste, or whatever, a T. R. Miller foreman assigned one of his to the job.

"At least that's how it worked when Tom Neal was involved," he added.

Gene directed the company's human resources department for thirty-three years, walking a tight-rope between the competing philosophies of Neal, the president, and John Richard Miller, both sons of original stake holders in the company's ownership. Neal thought the company should be community oriented, that whatever money was spent in charitable work and contributions was more than repaid in beneficent relations with the city. Miller wanted the company to take care of itself, its own business, wanted to put up a fence around the property, which he eventually did once Neal was leveraged out.

Gene didn't know the original source of the antagonism between the two. "But I'll give you an example of what I'm talking about," he said. For years he worked on an employee handbook, "Welcome to the company, meet your supervisor, that kind of thing." He'd draft a copy, take it to Miller, who'd dismiss the effort, tell him to start over.

"Then when Tom Neal saw me starting over on it, he'd ask why, and when I told him Mr. Miller said to, he'd say, 'Then forget the whole thing!' For years that went on," he said, chuckling.

"I remember I saw the employee handbook Hershey's used, you know, up in Pennsylvania, and I thought that was pretty good. So I modeled a version after theirs, took it to Mr. Miller, but he didn't like it, said it was 'too professional,'" Gene said, laughing even harder. "Told me to, 'stick to the chips and bark, son.'"

When a Chicago administrator was brought in to replace Neal in 1990, it wasn't long before Gene and most of the "Neal people" were gone, the company's largesse dried up, and the fence was erected.

Driving around the company's perimeter not long ago with Gene as a passenger, we ran into an unexpected dead end to what had been a frontage road, access now blocked. "See, that fence has cut off the town," he said.

By then the company owned 200,000 acres of land in Escambia and Conecuh counties. Ed Leigh McMillan, an early company attorney, shrewdly bought up as much land as possible in the 30s, 40s, and 50s. When oil was discovered beneath the land, it set the stage for future generations of Millers, Neals, and McMillans, once they reached adulthood, to receive monthly five-figure dividend checks. Those descendents would be amongst the last to endorse any effort to rewrite the constitution and have to surrender some of that money toward taxes and education. It wasn't one of their concerns.

"Here's another difference between Tom Neal and J.R. Miller," Gene said, not disguising his abiding allegiance. "Tom sent his boys to the public schools. Mr. Miller sent his away to a private boarding school."

"What didn't you like about Brewton?" I asked him.

"That kind of stuff, the snobbery of the elites."

"Or worse," Suzanne added, "the ones trying to claw their way into those circles."

"That's true," Gene said. "That was worse."

Murder Creek

Temple of Trees, Simmering Storm

THE DECISION TO investigate Annie Jean's story stemmed from an appearance at the Brewton Public Library upon the publication of Suzanne's novel. Of the book, Suzanne, said before its publication,

I was riding the back roads in West Alabama and Mississippi with a friend. He had been telling me about an old time radio disc jockey who had a religious program on the air that had not changed in decades. When he tuned in to what was supposed to be the program, he could only get this eerie rhythm of dead air. As a way of passing time, we began inventing a story of a deejay who goes missing in the middle of a broadcast, making up more characters, plotting out a story, which I started writing as soon as I got back home to Fish River. It wasn't working, though, until I added a much darker element from my own memory, something I had always wanted to revisit. I was somewhere around the age of eleven or twelve when this happened, and it stuck with me and disturbed me over the years.

Outside the small town where I grew up, a woman died under mysterious circumstances at a hunting camp house. There were lots of rumors, rumors of threats, and prominent names whispered around the community, but I never learned what really happened because it was all hushed up very quickly. Since I am not an investigative journalist or a detective, I have never attempted to look into the facts – if there are even any left available – as I always fantasized that I would. So this dark part of the book, enmeshed with the story of the phantom deejay, is not about that specific event, but rather, was inspired by it.

The "dark part" of the book involves a group of males, steeped in the hunting culture of rural Alabama, where men go through the bloody rituals of being initiated into the "kill club" alongside their gutted bucks and campfires, men who take on something of a "pack mentality" as they sexually use and abuse a young woman hired for their pleasure. Disturbing and violent, the victimization of the paid party girl, lumber mill worker Charity Collins, and the subsequent cover-up, echoes some of the theories and rumors surrounding the death of Annie Jean Barnes.

More than two hundred people attended the library event. In an ad run in the Standard prior to the engagement, borrowing a line from her grandfather, she told the publicist to instruct readers to "leave your dignity at home," in deference to those "darker" elements of the novel and in the hopes of making the event a casual, relaxed affair.

Nervous before any audience, she was additionally concerned about the old wounds she might have reopened, and who, exactly, would attend. Unbeknownst to her, in a central section of chairs fanned out before the lectern, sat five of the six adult children of Annie Jean Barnes who had remained in the Brewton area. Standing at the back of the room, having arrived a few minutes after she had begun, was someone else: George Perry Jr., son of the doctor who owned the camp house where Annie Jean was found battered and dazed decades earlier. He left the library before Suzanne concluded the question-and-answer portion of the agenda.

Outside after more than an hour of reading and signing books, Suzanne quickly found herself surrounded by the Barnes children. They had come for answers to the questions that have lingered all those years. But Suzanne could only assure them, "The book's not really about your mother. I just remember that story growing up and wanted to write about the kinds of people who would do such a thing. I didn't mean it as a portrayal of your mother at all."

Still, they questioned:

"What about your research?"

"Did you talk to Byrne, Taylor, hospital workers? What did they say?"

They told their versions of the story, the rumors that had circulated through the years, the discrepancies with what they had been told, their suspicions, and why. They were angry that someone could have gotten away with what happened to their mother, angry that, because she was poor and uneducated, the event could be hushed up so easily. The baby brother of the family stood off to the side of the discussion, sullen, muttering that he didn't want to have anything to do with the subject again. "Why can't you just leave it alone," he grumbled, a refrain that would be heard again and again, though tinged with various ulterior intent, from resignation to threatening. He did say, finally, that he would support whatever his brothers and sisters chose to do.

Able only to satisfy them by promising to find out what could still be discovered about the case, promising to return and listen to what they had to say, Suzanne then retreated to an isolated interior office of the library and broke down into tears.

At the time, she had pulled me into the contentious circle out there on the sidewalk for moral, if not physical, support. Later, at Willie's, with other friends and co-horts, I asked if she'd ever considered investigating the case, writing a non-fiction book.

"No," she answered, "I wouldn't know how to go about that, though now it seems like I should, you know? You saw them. You heard them."

"I wouldn't really know how to go about it either," I said, "other than asking a whole lot of questions. I can help you with that, if you like."

A few weeks after the library event, Suzanne attended a Brewton reading club's meeting at King David's former house, to discuss the book. But what was on everyone's mind was Annie Jean Barnes.

"The Brewton buzz," Suzanne's childhood friend Jamie Rutan said of the chatter, the same, thirty-seven year old chatter. Jamie's father, Wesley Gardner, had run the local radio station at the time, WEBJ—"that station with the hometown sound." He, like the editor at The Standard, had received threats to his life if he dared report or opine any further on the story. Now, Jamie's uncle, Hugh Caffey, a Harvard educated Brewton attorney, was saying of the book, in a Southern drawl tinged slightly with a New England brogue, "I don't know why Suzanne had to bring up that unfortunate incident again," though he hadn't actually read it.

"She says some of the original newspaper clippings have surfaced, that people are passing them around town," Suzanne told me.

"Amazing," I said, that a story could be severed like that, and yet, like a phantom limb, it's still there, just beyond visibility.

"She also says that the general attitude is 'why would this long forgotten incident be brought back up?'"

"Doesn't sound 'long forgotten' to me."

"We going to do this?" she asked.

"Got to."

We first contacted Annie Jean's eldest child, son Ralph, who lived in Biloxi, Mississippi. He was the only one of the siblings who had managed to extract himself from East Brewton, the wrong side of Murder Creek, via a stint in the Navy.

We met Ralph on a Saturday evening at the Waffle House in Biloxi. He is an animated, gray-haired, humorously self-deprecating man. He proceeded to tell us his version of the story, a version exceedingly true to the original rumors which had surfaced again, intact, with but a few variations, after all that time, the same version that was bandied about by the reading club, the same version once again infiltrating the dialogue of the entire town.

Annie Jean had gone to Dr. Perry's camp house that weekend to attend a party. Those private parties were notorious for the roll call of elite invitees, male scions of town who assembled for days of alcohol and poker and unrestrained debauchery. Any females in attendance, it was said, were there as party "favors," although Annie Jean was known to be Dr. Perry's girlfriend.

The best guess is that things simply got out of hand, though intimations of revenge, retaliation, silencing, even malicious disregard were also whispered. Ralph said he came home from a high school football game that Friday night about eleven o'clock. His mother had received a phone call earlier, and was waiting for a ride. His aunt Willie Mae was there, presumably to care for the children while Annie Jean was gone, though Ralph remembers the sisters arguing about whether Annie Jean should attend the party. Shortly thereafter Annie Jean was picked up. The phone call for help came less than thirty-six hours later, to the home of Mrs. Lovie Windham about 9:30 or 10:00, on Sunday morning, September 18, 1966. Her daughter was at the camp house of local physician Dr. George Perry, in the woods six miles north of Brewton.

Willie Mae decided the best course of action was to first get Jean away from the cabin and take her back home. Her brother, Buddy Windham, was then called to the house; after seeing the injuries, he contacted his physician, who ordered them to take her to the D. W. McMillan Hospital Emergency Room.

Six days later, after a period of slow but progressive recovery, Annie Jean "mysteriously" died on Saturday morning, September 24, 1966.

What happened?

The attending physician at the time, Dr. E. F. Strandell, reported that Annie Jean had been admitted with multiple contusions and abrasions, and a badly swollen left arm and right breast. She had multiple needle punctures and bruises on both arms. There were areas of her body that looked like they had been burned and other areas that looked as though the skin had been eroded. "She appeared to have been sexually assaulted but this will have to wait for the autopsy report."[11]

Dr. Strandell noted that Annie Jean's condition had improved during the week, that she was feeling better. Complicating her recovery was her apparent dependency on Demerol. Of that, Strandell said, "Her addiction had been controlled by much smaller doses of Demerol than she had been given prior to her admission."

On the morning of the 24th, "Annie Jean suddenly began gasping for breath. Nurses watched as her face turned blue. They summoned doctors, but in minutes she was dead."[12] Dr. Strandell theorized that a blood clot had killed her, and an autopsy was ordered to determine the exact cause of death.

Immediately following her death the circuit solicitor and the prosecuting attorney were notified. Both said that was the first they'd heard of Annie Jean's case, even though the sheriff's office was notified that previous Sunday when she was discovered and Federal agents were apprised of the event by family members the day after that. A state investigator, corporal Taylor, was called by the family on Friday the 23rd. His arrival in the hospital room marked the first attempt to interview Annie Jean by anyone other than Dr. Strandell.

She had first told everyone that she had fallen. But because her injuries were inconsistent with that explanation, Dr. Strandell questioned her further until she admitted to having been beaten. Corporal Taylor was told she'd been beaten that Friday. He then left Brewton on other business, with a promise to return and talk to Annie Jean after she'd fully recovered. Within hours she was dead.

Taylor did return, along with several other state investigators, to look into the case over the ensuing weeks. The Birmingham News, lead newspaper in Alabama's largest city, picked up the story a week after Annie Jean died, at the top of page one under the heading, "Mysterious Death of Young Divorcee Stirs Emotional Uproar in Brewton":

The strange case of Annie Jean Barnes has triggered the emotions of this Alabama town, correspondent Ted Pearson reported on location.

She was found in a lonely cabin badly beaten. Then she died.

Who beat her?

Did Annie Jean Barnes name her assailant before she died on a hospital bed to the satisfaction of investigators?

Is the guilty person still free because of allegations of "slipshod" law enforcement are founded? Or are the investigators plodding with slow and justified deliberation because so many angles need to be tied together?

These questions are on the lips of just about every single one of the nearly 10,000 residents in this city in South Alabama. No other incident or event in memory has stirred up such a local sensation.

"Whatever the immediate cause of death," Ted Pearson, the article's author wrote, "one certainty stands out: Annie Jean Barnes had been brutally beaten."

The family, he further reported, says Annie Jean was ready to "make and sign any statement" to clear up the mystery while in the hospital, but they had been unsuccessful in attempts to summon the local sheriff, Scotty Byrne, to her bedside. A state narcotics investigator, working an ongoing and widening drug case in the area, arrived in Brewton the day Annie Jean died, presumably at the hospital's behest. But Buddy Windham told Pearson he still possessed the Demerol and hypodermic equipment he had taken from his sister at their mother's house. He also said Annie Jean identified the source of the drug before she died. The authorities had not asked Windham about either issue.

Sheriff Byrne and District Attorney Wiley Henderson asked the state toxicologist to perform an autopsy, with a report promised two weeks after Pearson's article ran. The investigators would not say anything else about the case, pending the autopsy's report. Henderson is quoted as saying, "We're looking into the whole thing thoroughly. That's all I can say for the time being. Whatever I say at this point, I'm afraid, would be like throwing gasoline on the fire."[13]

That "fire" was articulated, "with all [his] journalistic indignation," Pearson noted, by the editor of the Brewton Standard, an editorial "assail[ing] the handling of the case by law enforcement":

It is with something akin to horror and almost an abject apology that we launch into what may well be one of the most appalling examples of slipshod law enforcement, of total unconcern for the vested interest of the public and of the apparent total lack of interest in the appeals of a private citizen for lawful protection of his rights.

The author, Tom Gardner, after listing a chronology of known facts, concluded by saying, "as tragic as the death of Ms. Barnes is, possibly it can serve to initiate an investigation to rid this community of much that is undesirable."[14] He signed the editorial, as did the newspaper's publisher, along with the radio station owner.

The October 6th edition of the Standard, a weekly publication, reported that more state investigators had moved into the case but in that week's editorial, Gardner backpedaled furiously, saving his tongue-lashing this time for the same private citizens of Brewton he had championed a week earlier. He chastised them for all the gossip and rumors circulating through town, even though every single letter from those citizens published on that same page whole-heartedly endorsed the call to "rid" their community of its "undesirable" elements. Strangely, the editorial concluded by reiterating that "no Brewton city police or FBI" were involved in the investigation.

The investigators went about their business, close-mouthed and tight-lipped. Two weeks later State Toxicologist Dr. Paul E. Shoffeitt fanned the flames to new heights by reporting his finding that Annie Jean Barnes died from "natural causes." Dr. Shoffeitt would make no other public comments despite the torrent of speculation and discontent that spread through the area concerning the handling of the case.

An Escambia Count Grand Jury convened as a matter of procedural routine. A month later they closed the book on the Annie Jean Barnes case, reporting to Circuit Judge Douglas Webb that "nothing was revealed" in the testimony heard from witnesses in the Barnes investigation "to warrant any action on the part of this body."

This is what that investigative body reported:

The grand jury spent considerable time hearing testimony from witnesses in connection with the investigation into the death of Annie Jean Barnes. It is the opinion of the grand jury that this case has been very thoroughly, completely and competently investigated.

All evidence having any bearing on the case was thoroughly investigated. All witnesses who wished to give testimony were permitted to do so, as well as many other witnesses who were subpoenaed as a result of the investigation by the various state investigators.

Dr. Paul E. Shoffeitt of the State Department of Toxicology performed the autopsy in this case, testified he could not pinpoint exactly the cause of death, and it is our opinion, based on the report of the investigators and the testimony of witnesses, that nothing was revealed which would warrant any action on the part of this body.

It was also the opinion and findings of the state investigators and of this grand jury that there is no evidence of any "payoff" to any official of Escambia County and no "coverup" of any evidence.

Dr. Strandell, who testified before the grand jury, left those proceedings saying to Annie Jean's family, "I can't believe they're getting away with this." Apparently, they were. Though there is this mild admonition of Sheriff Byrne included in the report:

This grand jury requests the court to advise the sheriff and his deputies that we believe, from evidence presented to this body, that there is a need for improvement in the methods used in the investigations performed by the sheriff's department into crimes or alleged crimes committed in this county. We believe that every citizen is entitled to a prompt, courteous and efficient investigation of their complaint. We also want to exonerate the sheriff personally, from any implication in any case brought before us. [15]

Buddy Windham and his twin brother left Brewton. Lovie Windham moved into a new home in East Brewton and assumed custody of Annie Jean's seven children, ranging in age from five to thirteen. The case was officially closed on November 18th when the Grand Jury recessed, and disappeared, some thought—and others hoped—forever.

"At the time," Ralph said, "the rumor was a maid who'd gone out there to clean up after the party had found mama outside the back door, naked, covered in fire ants, drug her back inside and made the phone call." While a maid, or anyone else unrelated, hadn't ever been mentioned in the newspaper accounts we'd seen, this was just the first in a long list of inconsistencies we would encounter among the remembered versions of the story.

Ralph knew that camp house well. It was a single storied building of wood and stone, set out in the woods, with a great room, kitchen, and bedrooms. Green, vertical clapboard outside, with a flat roof, and copious windows, the parking space is outside that back door which leads to the kitchen, and the bedrooms beyond. In the den, sat a couch, easy chairs, a recliner fanned around the open space, a fireplace recessed into a stone wall that wrapped around to an open aired barbecue pit. He had accompanied his mother on other visits to the place, when he would walk down the slope to boat house, pier, and pond to fish or throw rocks, or fish, while his mother was inside with Dr. Perry. Annie Jean was Dr. Perry's girlfriend—it was an open secret amongst the children and in town. He was nice to them, Ralph told us. One of the rumors circulating, again, had Mrs. Perry involved in the beating of her husband's "other woman."

The children were not allowed to see their mother, nor were they admitted to her hospital room. They did go to the courthouse during the grand jury deliberations, sitting outside the courtroom on long wooden benches, where they heard from Dr. Strandell after he exited the tall double doors, "Y'all might as well go on home. They're not going to do a goddamn thing about all this. I can't believe they're going to get away with it." Adding, according to the family, "You'll never know how much money was spent to bury this."

Ralph hadn't been able to squelch his indignation over the handling of the case through the years, and had returned to

Brewton on occasion while on leave from the military to try and get some answers. He went to Hugh Caffey's law office to find out what the attorney knew, how much he had been involved in the legal maneuverings, possibly even to seek advice or representation in his efforts.

"You need to just go on and leave it alone," was all Caffey would say to him, leaving Ralph feeling dismissed, inconsequential, and frustrated.

He went to McMillan Memorial Hospital, but was told his mother's medical records had burned in a storage warehouse fire some time back. (Neither Suzanne nor any others we talked with remembered such a warehouse, let alone a fire.) He stormed into Dr. Perry's office on another occasion, warning the doctor, "I'm not that little boy anymore," demanding answers. No answers were forthcoming, though the flustered, apologetic Perry did try to assure Ralph how much he'd cared for Annie Jean.

"I don't care what you find out about my mother," Ralph said, pledging his support, "if it means getting to the truth, and someone pays for what they did to her." He was well aware of the high-brow impressions of Annie Jean Barnes, that she was nothing but a white trash drug addict who attached herself to a doctor who would support her habit. Ralph, to the contrary, remembered her as warm, fun-loving, almost goofy, all the time joking with the children, a woman with an effervescent, contagious personality. "She was more like my friend than my mother," he said, remembering times she'd taken him honky-tonking to the White Horse, a roadside tavern just north of Brewton, not too far before the turn-off to Dr. Perry's camp house. He would sit at a table inside sipping bottles of Coca-Cola while Annie Jean danced, and flirted, and partied.

Club White Horse has been described as "a roadhouse with good steaks." It's a non-descript cinder block building, its few windows painted over, pebbled parking space along the front and both sides, at the crest of a curving rise in 31 that makes it "a challenge," navigating late-night exits and entrances, which not everyone succeeded. Up on the flat roof, a white neon horse, modeled after the White Horse Scotch logo, stands vigilant.

Inside, you could find a cross-section of the town, elites over in a corner, a long central table full of "rednecks and whores." The White Horse, it's said, was "the place to go and let it all hang out," where everyone was welcomed to the beer, the steaks, a turn on the dance floor, swaying to whatever was pouring out of the juke box—everyone—the elites, the rednecks, the whores, even an Annie Jean Barnes of East Brewton.

The same picture of Annie Jean accompanied articles in different newspapers covering the story. She is standing in profile, her light hair pulled back, worn short, off of her impish face. Her left shoulder, bared in a sleeveless cotton shirt faces the camera. She is looking at the picture-taker through the corners of her narrowed eyes, an almost imperceptible turn to her mouth, the very beginning of a grin, as if she had just been caught initiating some prank and was readying to enlist the cameraman as an accomplice in her devious plan rather than abandon it. The picture is an embodiment of the verbal portrait Ralph painted of his mother, where you can see the playfulness, and all but hear the snicker bubbling inside her somewhere.

Spent by the painful and frustrating memories, Ralph gave us the phone number of two of his sisters, who lived in the other Brewton suburb of Alco. We promised to keep in touch.

Murder Creek

Alco, Alabama

THE SISTERS, BRENDA and Joyce, lived on Franklin Street, west of 31 and past the Jefferson Davis Community College Campus. A little farther down 31 is Craver's Funeral Home. The area is also, ironically, where Dr. Perry's "office" used to be. An old saying in town held that to get to Doc Perry's, you have to go by Craver's.

Speculation about the reasons for Perry's relatively remote office location—the Perry home was a few miles to the north, very near the First United Methodist Church, the rest of Brewton's elites, and the only hospital in town—runs the gamut. One says he was shunned by Brewton's medical community, either because he had come from poverty, because of his shady personal habits (his affairs, reported drug and alcohol abuse) or some combination of the two. Another suggests that it was Perry who avoided those social and professional circles: both he and his wife were said to live relatively insular lives, eschewing the church and societal organizations typical of small Southern communities. Regardless, it is known that he practiced out of McMillian hospital at one time and then moved that practice to a converted house in Alco under an unspecified cloud at some point. One of his former patients, an East Brewton resident, remembers that Perry was known, on that side of the creek, to be a doctor who wouldn't turn away poorer patients. He also remembers Perry drinking while he was treating them. Perry was found dead and alone—his wife Marguerite having divorced him some years earlier, his two children having left Brewton immediately upon graduating high school—having succumbed to a lifetime of abuse, in 1979.

That same year saw the first in a string of unsolved murders in the area. Some started calling Brewton "Murder City," fulfilling the prophecy saddled upon the city back in 1966, in the midst of the Barnes case, when Brewton was labeled as "Little Phenix

Murder Creek

City."* Timothy Baber was found murdered near the Brewton airport in October, 1979. Rumors fluttered around this case, too, from a jealous friend, to a drug deal gone south, to a more officious hit: his ex-wife said, confessing her fear of the danger he was courting through his alleged drug running, only weeks before his death at age 29, that he reassured her by saying, "Don't worry. I know all the right people."

Two and a half years later a definite execution took place in the woods near the White Horse. About 2:30 on a Sunday afternoon in April, J. D. Davidson parked his taxi, sat there an undetermined amount of time, though long enough for a smoke, it seems, as cigarette butts were found at the scene—from two different brands—before he was shot three times: once in the back, twice in the head. Then the car was set on fire. No one was ever convicted in either case, though local law enforcement officials have always been implicated in both, in the minds of some residents. One of whom, Baber's ex, casually remarked as late as 2006, "Oh yeah. If you want someone killed, come to Brewton."

In early 1987, an East Brewton girl, Vickie Lynn Pittman, disappeared one Friday evening, only to turn up brutally murdered some weeks later. No one was convicted in that case either, despite a short list of likely suspects and a laundry list of

---

* As noted in an October 20, 1966, editorial in the *Brewton Standard*: "The good name of Brewton has been battered around in recent weeks from one end of the state to another..." including the above, dubious sobriquet: Phenix City is infamous for the Albert Patterson assassination detailed in the excellent book, *When Good Men Do Nothing*, and as the place Patton threatened to flatten with his tank brigade because of the ill-reputed effect the town's many vices were having on his troops—returning from furloughs with VD!—who would venture there from Ft. Benning, across the river in Columbus, Georgia, against orders.

evidence including a vehicle, boots soiled from the crime scene, clothing of the deceased, knowledge of her burial place out in the woods, and a confession. The investigation stopped short, however, of nailing down a probable motive, because one of those suspects was a star state's witness in the rigged trial of Johnny D. McMillan for the murder of Rhonda Morrison in Monroeville a few months earlier. McMillan., falsely accused, and convicted—against overwhelming evidence to the contrary—was sentenced to death in Alabama's electric chair, the "Yellow Mama." It took years to get the phony conviction overturned and Johnny released, and when he was set free from Holman prison in 1993, that added another name to Alabama's cold case files.

Brewton is not alone in this, obviously. Nor is Alabama. There are unsolved murders in nearly every jurisdiction, no doubt. The Morrison/Pittman cases do illustrate a particularly egregious aspect of life in Alabama, though, if you're poor, anyway. What started as an attempt to disfranchise the state's blacks in September 1901, and then its poor whites incrementally in the succeeding years, resulted in those partially represented citizens being viewed as only partially deserving of any of the rights and privileges afforded other, fully entitled members of the society. Is there any real wonder, then, when that institutionalized sense of privilege and entitlement turns malignant in some of those who deem themselves more worthy and deserving than others— because, constitutionally, they are—that the murder of a teen-aged girl in East Brewton doesn't garner the same priority, legally, judicially, as the murder of a higher-classed teenager in Monroeville? Or that a drug dealer or a cabbie can be summarily rubbed out? Or that a poor young woman from the lowest of that pecking order, who dared to cross that line, perhaps, could be beaten and left for dead?

Pete Earley, author of Circumstantial Evidence: Death and Justice in a Southern Town, about the Morrison and Pittman cases, framed the question this way:

One night when she was watching the national news on television, a network correspondent appeared on the screen, standing on the steps of the U.S. Supreme Court in Washington. Mozelle [Pittman's aunt] had not been paying much attention to the newscast until that moment, but she suddenly found herself leaning forward, peering at the screen. Right above the reporter's head, chiseled in stone across the screen, were the words EQUAL JUSTICE UNDER LAW. Was that what Vickie Lynn was getting? (p. 128)

In the book, Bryan Stevenson, the new director for the Alabama Capital Representation Resource Center, is the lawyer who took on McMillan's case, and ultimately gained his freedom. He told Earley,

The problem is that too many people in the justice system define their contribution as being like a modern-day Atticus Finch. Well, that is not enough! What you should care about is creating a society and a legal system where people are not forced to have an Atticus Finch represent them, where people who do not have enough money or who are black or who are not well educated do not have to be in a position where they pray for an Atticus Finch to step forward.

What I am talking about is the next level up from To Kill a Mockingbird, a higher level where what Atticus Finch did is not seen as extraordinary but as normal – the everyday way that things should be done. That is the level where the people in the margins are made part of the entire community, and that not only benefits the invisible people but also the community. It makes for a better community because it makes for real justice. (p. 331)

Murder Creek

There is one other sensational murder locals bring up when discussing the subject. In October, 1988: Stephanie King was abducted from the Alco Baptist Church, not far from Franklin Street, raped, and strangled. Edward Russell Dubose was convicted for the crime in 1989 and sentenced to death, but that conviction was also overturned, because the defense was not afforded an opportunity to refute DNA evidence introduced. Dubose later pleaded guilty in a 1997 retrial and is serving a life sentence today.

A lot like the Morrison murder two years earlier, there was some speculation that Dubose, a black man, 29 at the time, wasn't the murderer. The problem with all these murders is that they're local affairs, and as such, in a town like Brewton, or Monroeville, or countless other small towns, the participants, all the participants, are familiar people, folks likely to be repeatedly encountered in the course of a work day, at a restaurant, or in church. There's a significant difference, as Earley points out in the preface to his book, when such affairs take place in larger cities. There, often, high-profile lawyers, or defendants, or victims, become the story, often a separate story, because of their personal notoriety. Not so, he suggests, in a small town. When the names have faces, faces of people you've grown up with, live or work beside, the story never goes away, no matter the outcome. Because of that there is considerable pressure to resolve the issue correctly, but there is also an impetus to resolve it quickly. That alone creates enough margin for error, that onus of haste. When the rumored participants happen to be local scions, where reputations and careers are at risk, it is easy to become suspicious when a defenseless—at least defense-handicapped—person is accused, or victimized, and the case disappears altogether, like Annie Jean's, disappears through the cracks in the justice system, at least. As we found out, the story was anything but "long forgotten."

Murder Creek

Unlike the Dubose case, DNA was not an issue in 1966, of course. An investigator on the Barnes case has said, "We didn't even know what that was back in those days." He can hardly be faulted for that. Not many people knew that much about DNA in 1966. Watson and Crick had only published their model in scientific journals in 1953, for which they won the 1962 Nobel Prize. It wasn't until Watson's The Double Helix, in 1968, that the discovery found a wider audience. That same investigator, now retired, went on to say, "I hope you find something, I really do. There are questions that haven't been answered. They," the family, "deserve to find out what happened, if you can find it," when he was finally contacted about the case.

The anger and frustration from not knowing what happened thirty-seven years after the case was palpable in the living room of the small house on Franklin Street, back in Alco, a blue-collar suburb south of Brewton. Sisters Joyce and Brenda sat in the room, accessed through the garage and a side screened door, both welcoming and yet fairly seething at the same time. The room was crowded with furniture. Dogs came and went, pushing and pulling on the door for themselves, the noise of the hatch slapping shut the only sound for a few awkward moments, while the women collected themselves and organized their thoughts. They were upset as much by the story surfacing again, as by the story itself. Or they were conflicted, and grappling with that conflict, that it was still, essentially, the same, incomplete story. Their frustration was initially and importantly evident in the fact that they didn't even have an adequate term to name what had happened. They couldn't call it a "murder" or a "homicide." The grand jury had prevented them from pursuing either of those, even though, as New York State Chief Judge Sol Wachtler quipped in a 1985 interview, a prosecutor could—because grand jury proceedings are so heavily stacked in the prosecution's favor— "indict a ham sandwich." Was it an accident? Annie Jean's insurance underwriter didn't think so, as her accidental policy was never paid to the family. Was it really just an "unfortunate incident," as Mr. Caffey has characterized it?

The sisters saved most of their anger for the sheriff at the time, Gladin Scott "Scotty" Byrne. Byrne was first chastised, then exonerated, in the Grand Jury report. He had been Escambia County sheriff since 1959, and would serve many more years in that capacity. In the end, it's been said, you couldn't go anywhere in the state of Alabama (or Georgia, for that matter) where you wouldn't run into someone who knew Scotty Byrne.

"He was out there, you know," Brenda said. "That morning Aunt Willie found mama."

"Why?"

"Never said."

"What did she say?"

"Aunt Willie? She won't talk about it."

"Gets mad at us if we even ask," Joyce said. "Didn't speak to me at all for a long time the last time I asked her about it."

Another relative had recently told them, though, that Willie Mae might finally be willing to discuss her sister's death, now that she was older, her health failing. "Everyone always said mama told her who beat her up like that."

"And there's that story about what happened the morning she died," Brenda added.

The story, they said, is that Willie Mae was at Annie Jean's bedside the morning she died, quietly visiting. She was summoned out to the nurse's station in the hallway, for a phone call.

"But there was no one on the phone."

She returned to the room to find the nurses watching her sister struggle for air, with the doctors on their way, though they would be too late.

Joyce, later, and with some difficulty, summoned some happier memories of her mother. Though she was only eight years old when Annie Jean died, Joyce, like Ralph, remembers her mom as playful, mischievous. "She would come home from work, park the car at the end of the driveway, come inside and herd us all out into the car. She'd say, 'Who wants to go for a ride?' Then she'd start the car up and pull into the driveway, laughing at the prank she'd pulled. That was our 'ride'."

Other times when she came home from work, especially payday Fridays, Annie Jean gave each of the kids a quarter to go to the corner store for candy. And still another time, Joyce remembers Annie Jean's old Ford stalling out at a railroad crossing in town, everyone spilling from the clunker to push it off the tracks before the next freight train rumbled through. She remembers at least three or four moves from one ramshackle rental to another in the same squalid neighborhood of East Brewton, from Dailey Street, to Gillis Street, to Victory, in those eight years—lateral moves, at best, to hear descriptions of the area.

She doesn't, she said, remember Annie Jean and Fred Barnes, Joyce's father, ever being together. Annie Jean left East Brewton, with her baby Ralph, right after graduating high school in 1954. Looking for work, she met and married Fred, birthing twins Linda and Brenda in 1956, daughter Theresa in '57, Joyce in '58, Fred in '59, and finally Lonnie in 1962, all the while following Fred from Alabama to Georgia to Ohio, and Texas, after he'd moved on ahead of the family, looking for work—painting, mostly—but ultimately unable to hold down job after job. It was in Texas in 1962 where Fred was arrested and jailed, when Annie Jean finally left him and moved with her children back to East Brewton, and took up with Dr. Perry.

Fred was little more than a phantom in Joyce's life after that, though she does remember the family starting out on a trip to Greenville, Mississippi, to see him once, only to be truncated a short while later by an accident near Monroeville. All she can say about him now is that he died sometime in the early eighties, and is buried "somewhere in Georgia."

Joyce's life is a repetition of her mother's, in many respects, even if she has improved on the model. She married young, and became a mother young. She is now a single grandparent, of children from yet another broken home. Joyce owns the house on Franklin Street, and is justifiably proud of that. She works hard—at the Gray Goose bar down near the state line in Atmore, or closer to town, at the Hog Heaven BBQ place—always has, and will readily say that her children always had food, and clothing, just as, she says, her grandchildren will. But there is little joy in her face, a face that is open and trusting, younger looking than her years—when she relaxes, that is. There's something missing, an absence quantifiably different from any lack of a luxurious lifestyle or a satisfying career. It's something bigger, more meaningful, more painful, a gap she's powerless to do much about, other than carry it around on her shoulders, and in her thoughts and dreams.

As we drove out of Brewton that day I was reminded of Suzanne's line that nothing has changed in Brewton, "except more Pizza Huts..."

And I wondered, How is that possible, that they could be so incontrovertibly stuck?

Murder Creek

Malfeasance, Alabama

BUT THE REAL question is, exactly how did it become like that? How could the ridiculously rich look out their back doors down on the paltry existence of Brewton's hopelessly poor without some bite of conscience, some sense of injustice? Was this really a reasonable picture of 20th century America, after all the efforts of the New Deal and the Great Society, regardless of whatever shortcomings those programs had? How had Brewton, as well as much of Alabama, actually, been left behind? The answers seemed to be more than a century old.

The delegates elected to the constitutional convention in Montgomery swore an oath to "support the Constitution of the United States," and to "honestly and faithfully perform"[16] their duties as delegates, on May 21, 1901. Those 155 delegates — mostly white conservative Democrats, mostly lawyers, with no women, and no blacks — who signed the roll that day, produced a document three and a half months later, whose faithfulness, integrity, and fairness has been challenged ever since. By the end of the twentieth century, surviving no less than eight campaigns to severely ratify or replace it altogether, the Alabama State Constitution was the nation's oldest, largest, most complex and least effective such document. Today, it is the longest constitution in the world. The sad result of that was, and remains, the fact that Alabama's citizens have very little, if any, control of their government, which was the expressed objective of those who controlled that 1901 delegation.

The architects of the constitution had no qualms whatsoever about expressing their original intent. On every envelope sent out by the Alabama Democratic State Campaign Committee urging members to ratify the constitution was printed what's been generously called a "curious modification" of America's motto, e

60

pluribus unum: "White Supremacy, Honest Elections, and the New Constitution One and Inseparable."

Wayne Flynt, a man who has been identified by those who continue the fight for a new state constitution as one of the best candidates to author a new governing document, probably knows as much about the subject as anyone, which is no small achievement. One of the chief complaints concerning the 1901 Constitution, at this juncture at least, is that it is all but incomprehensible. Michael Allen and Jamison Hinds offer this comparison: "The genius of the U.S. Constitution, in part, is its simplicity. The U.S. Constitution is studied by high school government classes, while there are only a few scholars in Alabama who can navigate the intricacies of Alabama's governing documents."[17] Flynt is one of those scholars. Much of what follows about the events leading up to the 1901 constitutional convention is taken from his *Alabama in the Twentieth Century* (University of Alabama Press, 2004).

"Before the Civil War virtually all white Alabamians farmed for a living," Flynt writes—the agrarian society de Toqueville reported on—and saw no need to encourage any other form of revenue, such as manufacturing, banking, or business. The governor routinely "rejected requests by private entrepreneurs for state subsidies to help build roads, canals, railroads, or other economic infrastructure."

Some other wealthier and better-educated Alabamians, though, were "receptive to higher taxes and government inducements encouraging business," and this first opened societal fissures along political and class lines. Jacksonian Democrats were suspicious of any government activity or intrusion into their lives, while Republicans "were more supportive of business." But "no whites, of any class, believed that blacks should participate fully in government or society."[18] That all changed with the "war between the states," as they refer to it in Alabama, and Reconstruction.

"Freedmen began to vote, hold public office, and draft laws." Along with their "white Republican allies, they paid taxes, levied taxes, and dispersed the proceeds. They offered state financial inducements to private business" and favored increases in public services, especially education. "With slavery ended and luxuries greatly reduced, they shifted the primary burden of taxation from affluent planters to struggling yeoman farmers,"[19] who cursed the Reconstruction government for its inclusion of former slaves as well as its taxation strategies, the "corrupting agent" of "expanding capitalism" Williams wrote about.*

Another war ensued over the next ten years "until white conservative Democrats regained control of government in 1874" and resorted to ever increasing forms of political corruption throughout the last quarter of the century to maintain that control. The 1875 constitution prohibited the state from loaning money or extending credit for internal improvements. They capped state and local property taxes, segregated schools, abolished the state Board of Education, and employed a variety of strategies to dilute black representation. They gerrymandered maps, made state and local offices appointive rather than elective, and complicated election laws. Only threats of federal intervention kept that convention from going as far as they would twenty-six years later, and those measures fell short of their objective. By "1900 more than 100,000 African Americans" were eligible to vote, and "along with their white allies during the 1890s Populist insurrection,"[20] created intolerable mischief.

---

* Interestingly, at about he same time, the Agrarians yearned for a return to that pre-war society in *I'll Take My Stand* (1930).

Populists terrified conservative Democrats, especially in the Black Belt, where wealthy landowners feared a neo-Reconstruction coalition gaining power and imposing higher taxes. In 1892, and again in 1894, "planters had to steal black votes in the Black Belt in order to deny Populist leader Reuben Kolb the governorship." Coming into 1900, whites knew something had to be done. "The U.S. senatorial race in Alabama that year became a referendum on suffrage, with the incumbent U.S. senator arguing for a disfranchisement" convention to rewrite the state's constitution and "the sitting governor opposing both disfranchisement and constitutional revision." The proconvention incumbent won and 60 percent of polled voters supported the call for a convention.

"Of the 155 delegates elected to the 1901 constitutional convention, 141 were Democrats, 7 were Populist, 6 Republican, and 1 independent. Ninety-six of the delegates were lawyers and 12 were bankers. No Negroes or women were elected."[21]

Anniston railroad lawyer John B. Knox presided over the convention. Knox's presidential address to the delegates unambiguously stated the primary agenda of the gathering. "And what is it that we want to do?" he asked. "Why it is within the limits imposed by the Federal Constitution, to establish white supremacy in this State. This is our problem, and we should be permitted to deal with it, unobstructed by outside influences, with a sense of our responsibilities as citizens and our duty to posterity." Those "outside influences," of course, were the result of "Northern Interference," which Knox clarifies as "not so much to elevate the black man as it is to humiliate the white man with whom they have been in antagonism." He then reassures his audience – all male, all white – that "the Southern man knows the negro, and the negro knows him. The only conflict which has, or is ever likely to arise, springs from the effort of ill-advised friends in the North to confer upon him, without previous training or preparation, places of power and responsibility, for which he is wholly unfitted, either by capacity or experience," the last thirty years notwithstanding. Finally, in a perversion of Constitutional reform, he implored the delegates, "But if we would have white supremacy, we must establish it by law – not by force or fraud.... These provisions are justified in law and in morals, because the negro is not discriminated against on account of his race, but on account of his intellectual and moral condition. There is a difference, it is claimed with great force, between the uneducated white man and the ignorant negro. There is in the white man an inherited capacity for government, which is wholly wanting in the negro." Knox ended his presidential address with the proclamation, "I do not doubt that you will discharge" your responsibilities "with courage and fidelity," and a non-sequitur reference to an Old Testament parable, in which Abou Ben Adhem beseeches and angel to "write me as one who loves his fellow man."[22]

Except, Mr. Knox had just iterated for the convention why the "ignorant negro"—as well as the "uneducated white man", come to find out—was not, in his estimation, a "fellow man," and as such was not deserving of love, or protection, suffrage, or any other benefit of society or governance. Now, having grown up as one of Knox's "ill-advised friends in the North," I didn't have the same experience with the "problem" in the South, and so would cede the notion that it was theirs to fix, unobstructed. One would have hoped, though, for a point of parliamentary procedure at that juncture, that at least one delegate would have stepped forward to ask what proof Knox could offer for those assumptions, what evidence could be entered into the record. Because they didn't come from anything like scientific or even sociological fact, obviously.

There is a founding document covering the subject, however, in the form of a letter delivered to James River Colony, Virginia, plantation owners in 1712 by a British West Indies slave owner, Willie Lynch—from whom the racially scorching term "lynching" is derived—entitled, "The Making of a Slave."* In it Lynch details a process he says utilizes "the same basic principle that we use in breaking a horse, combined with some more sustaining factors," which included stripping the Alpha male, tar and feathering him, tying him to two horses, setting him on fire, whipping the horses to tear him in half, and then bullwhipping the others, all in the interests of "good economics." The goal of the process was to psychologically and emotionally cripple the slave population, denying their humanity, if only because such torture, abuse and manipulation could be levied without redress, without any possibility of justice. (Consider this: the pre Civil War prison population in Alabama was 99% white and changed nearly overnight to a post-war population that was 90% black. Why? Because blacks accused of a crime were simply turned over the plantation owners to mete out any punishment they wanted.) The process worked so well that in 1832 Henty Berry proclaimed before the Virginia House of Delegates, "We have, as far as possible, closed every avenue by which light may enter their [the slaves'] minds. If we could extinguish the capacity to see the light our work would be complete; they would then be on a level with the beasts of the field and we should be safe."[23]

Freedmen were just a different brand of animal, in the minds of the convention conferees, that could still be manipulated, abused, broken, disfranchised and dehumanized, still in the interests of "good economics." Spread the agenda to include Alabama's "white trash," a Southern Americanism that doesn't surface until the 1850s, in response to, an attempt to distract from, perhaps, the mounting cries for abolition, and then those Big Mules and planters could really "be safe."

---

* The letter, some three hundred years later is shockingly graphic, unambiguously repugnant, and, coincidentally, mostly ignorant.

Flynt segregates the delegation into four different contingents. "The weakest delegation contained Populist remnants," who "could do little more than wage a rearguard action against those seeking to disfranchise poor whites." A slightly larger group of "Progressives expressed support for humanitarian causes, clean government, better funding for schools, expanded public services, antilynching legislation, and prison reforms. The two groups that dominated the proceedings though were planters and "Big Mules." Planters were large landowners most prevalent in the Black Belt. Big Mules represented the state's banks, railroads, and industries, and were centered in the Birmingham district, a belt of industrial towns across the northern part of the state from Anniston and Gadsden to Tuscaloosa."[24] They were the coalition that elected Knox and controlled most other aspects of the proceedings.

"With their purpose clearly stated, and any possible opposition either unrepresented or divided, the planter-Big Mule coalition" went to work. "Suffrage restriction had driven the call for the convention and dominated debate. With no African American delegates and almost non-existent support for them from any white faction, blacks had no way of protecting themselves from disfranchisement." The main question became whether blacks would be the sole target of the restrictive strategies or "whether delegates would add poor whites as secondary casualties of a process transferring all governmental power into 'the hands of the intelligent and virtuous.'"[25]

Clearly, there was precious little debate on the issue. "Some delegates among the predominant coalition left little doubt about their objective. To them, poor white Populists – the great unwashed, uneducated masses of white tenant farmers; textile, steel, and sawmill workers; coal and iron ore miners – were as much a threat to their class hegemony as were black voters." Blacks at least "knew their place" within the social and political hierarchy. The greater threat came from uppity whites. "Former governor William C. Oates, a near political casualty of the earlier Populist insurrection, maintained that 'there are some white men who have no more right to vote than a negro and not as much as some of them'." Newspapers in Alabama's major cities consented, for the most part, though the Populist Tuscaloosa American noted presciently, "past history teaches us that the rule of the so-called 'virtuous and intelligent,' the rule of the rich and the favored has ever been one of the most tyrannical and despotic. Under such rule, but two classes exist, the master and the slave."

The suffrage provisions of the new constitution spelled out that rule. "Residency requirements of two years in the state and one year in the county were aimed at tenant farmers and industrial workers. The poll tax of $1.50 per year, cumulative if unpaid to a maximum of $36, effectively struck down both white and black tenants…. Crimes that disqualified voters included not only felonies such as murder, rape, and robbery, but also homosexuality, bigamy, adultery, vagrancy, hoboing," and "moral turpitude." The "most obvious intent of the delegates could be found in the property requirement. In a state with ever increasing numbers of yeoman farmers losing their land to mortgage foreclosures or inability to pay property taxes, the constitution required that registrants own 40 acres of land with all taxes paid or $300 worth of personal property,"[26] a thinly veiled sarcastic coda, no doubt, to Lincoln's promised ideal of emancipation vis-a-vis the realities of life in Alabama. What Knox called "wise scheme[s] for the regulation of the right of suffrage, and for the purification of the ballot,"[27] essentially reconstituted, along with Mississippi, Georgia, South Carolina and Louisiana, a democratically rebellious confederacy, salvaging the "lost cause."

If there was any legitimately democratic aspect of the process, it would only be the provision to ratify it, what turned out to be just another veil. "The constitution was completed on September 3rd. Delegates provided for a public referendum on November 11 during state elections. . . . The debate during September, October, and November focused nearly exclusively on race. Pro-ratification forces adopted a simple mantra: 'White supremacy, suffrage reform and purity in elections.' . . . The Birmingham Age-Herald argued that a vote for legal disfranchisement was a vote for lower taxes, economical government, better schools, and white supremacy, and against the political corruption that had been required to control black voters. 'What is most wanted for the general good,' the editor summarized, 'is assured white supremacy.'

"Paradoxically the constitution that was intended to eliminate electoral corruption in Alabama was adopted by the very corruption it was designed to end. The vote to ratify carried by a count of 108,613 to 81,734. Thirty-four counties went for ratification, 32 against. The vote in 54 counties was 76,263 against ratification to 72,389 in favor. The victory margin came from 12 Black Belt counties with a Negro population of more than two-thirds that reported late returns. The vote in those 12 counties was 36,224 to ratify and 5,471 against. Dallas, Hale, and Wilcox counties cast 17,475 votes for the constitution and only 508 against, or 12,360 more than the total white male voting population, assuming that every white male voted and every one favored ratification. So much for the 'purity of elections' ratifiers had promised."[28]

The truth is, "The organic law that governed Alabama during the 20th century was, like the political process that created it, stained with racism and corruption." And the architects were "Alabama's finest, wealthiest, and self-proclaimed 'best' citizens. In 1905 John B. Knox, president of the 1901 convention, conceded that for all the talk of ridding politics of the Negro, the objective of the convention had really been 'to place the power of government in the hands of the intelligent and virtuous.'"[29]

The most egregious result of the new law was precisely that which those power-mongers most desired, a precipitous decline in voting. "In 1900 approximately 181,000 negro voters had been eligible under the old 1875 constitution. By January 1, 1903, only 2,980 had been permitted to register under the new. Particularly dramatic was the decline in the Black Belt, where Negro registration in 14 counties declined from 79,311 to 1,081.

"Among white voters the decline was less dramatic but still substantial.... Some 25,000 to 50,000 who registered did not pay their poll tax during the first year," hence becoming ineligible to vote. "And as decades passed, the effect of the poll tax became more punitive and exclusionary because of the accumulative feature that required voters to pay it every year from age 21 to 45 whether or not there was an election (a constitutional feature shared only by Georgia). When the Alabama Policy Institute studied voter participation in 1941-42, it estimated that some 600,000 whites and 520,000 negroes were disfranchised by various provisions of the 1901 constitution. In most counties more whites were disfranchised than registered, limiting the vote to a select elite. Negroes remained totally shut out of participation in their own government despite the fact that some of them were at that very moment fighting in the armed services to protect it.

"By the middle of the century Alabamians would 'grouse' about low turnout for elections. Yet that was precisely the intent and effect of the state's constitution. In 1900 153,300 voters cast ballots in the gubernatorial election. Six years later only 94,700 voted in the highly contentious 1906 governor's race, nearly a 40 percent decline despite a population increase. In presidential elections Alabama's turnout declined from 34 percent in 1900 to 21 in 1904 and 14 in 1924. In the decade before 1900, as many as 80 percent of eligible Alabamians, white and black, voted. In 1940 only a third of adults were even registered.

"What makes the 1901 suffrage provisions even more significant is comparison with the state's first constitution. Otherwise one might assume that the operative principle in

Alabama public policy had always been anti-democratic. Actually, the opposite was true. The 1819 constitution, which ushered Alabama into the Union, was a projection of the towering presence of Thomas Jefferson and the democratic aspirations of the American Revolution. Delegates to that convention had pointedly refused to restrict suffrage based on literacy, ownership of property, or even church affiliation. Any white male 21 years of age or older could vote, whether or not he could read, write, owned property, belonged to a church or even believed in God. But the democratic assumptions of that first gathering of founding fathers at Huntsville in July 1819 were not shared by their successors in Montgomery in the summer of 1901. And it would take the federal government to step in and restore some semblance of democracy to the state…. It was Congress in the 1965 Voting Rights Act that finally enfranchised Alabama blacks. And it was the U.S. Supreme Court in 1966 that ensured the right to vote for all the state's poor of whatever color when it struck down the poll tax,"[30] the year Annie Jean Barnes died.

Murder Creek

Prattville, Alabama

PRATTVILLE IS LITTLE more than the splash of Montgomery's retired and relatively affluent that seeped north and west of the city, as interstate 65 coursed that way toward Birmingham. The three exits off of I-65 for Prattville, once it crosses the Alabama River over the American Legion bridge, boast typical clusters of franchise hotels, fast-food outlets, and gas stations, fireworks palaces and antique galleries, indistinguishable from just about any other interstate exit, in Alabama, at least. Off of those immediate thoroughfares, though, tucked away in a brochure neighborhood, lives retired Alabama Bureau of Investigation Captain R. C. "Pete" Taylor. As the initial lead state investigator on the Barnes case, Taylor was the first most logical source of information that might provide some answers toward filling that gap in Joyce's life. It wouldn't be easy, though.

We actually first tried to track down Ned Pearson, the Birmingham News correspondent who'd been reporting from the scene, but no one knew where he was. Through those efforts, though, we were given the name of Ken Hallford, the director of Alabama's Bureau of Investigation, and it was from Hallford that we learned about Captain Taylor.

I called Captain Taylor in December 2003, told him what we were doing, said we'd like to talk to him sometime, and asked if that would be possible.

"Sure," he said. "Send me some information about you, what you're interested in, and why."

We sent him a copy of Suzanne's book, along with brief sketches about us and the project. I then initiated an email exchange with him to try and arrange a meeting. Some weeks later he answered, requesting some sample questions and dates that would be convenient for us to travel north.

We were just interested in what he remembered about the investigation, I told him, and the grand jury proceedings. "There's been a lot of talk about Sheriff Byrne's role in the case, as you probably know," I said. "We'd welcome your appraisal of that."

The first good opportunity to interview Taylor came in February, 2004, as Suzanne had a book engagement scheduled in LaGrange, Georgia, midday on the 19th, not far from Montgomery. "Would you be available later that afternoon, or the next morning?" I asked.

He said he'd look at his schedule, but thought it was open, that we could meet in Montgomery, where his old case files were stored.

"Whichever time is best for you," I answered.

But on the 17th I received an email from him saying he wouldn't be able to meet us after all. His wife was having some difficulty with her back and they were scheduled to meet with a specialist later in the week.

That pattern was repeated over the next twelve months; suggested dates when we'd be traveling through or around the area, preliminary scheduling, then cancellation.

In the meantime, through a high school friend of Suzanne's, we were able to obtain a portion of the Alabama Department of Toxicology report submitted to Sheriff Byrne on October 21, 1966. The first thing we noticed was that Dr. Shoffeitt, the assistant director and medical examiner on record, was not a medical doctor, according to the letterhead on the report, but a Ph.D.

"Ph.D in what?" Suzanne asked.

"Doesn't say. Could be anything, though presumably it's in the health sciences."

"That's odd."

"Sure is. I always thought pathologists did autopsies."

Nelson Grubbs, a toxicologist in Mobile, performed the laboratory examination of the materials submitted by the investigators from the cabin. He found a bedspread labeled "from floor" completely wet with urine. Another bedspread, "from bed," had one small blood stain and green grass stains. A blue sheet had three inch-and-a-half blood stains and light, streaked blood stains leading toward the edge of the sheet. A white uniform, "washed," with grass stains. A white, padded brassiere with clips at the upper edge of the cup and another on the strap, were consistent with positions of injuries noted in pictures of the body of Mrs. Barnes, the report said. Other clothing submitted by Sheriff Byrne, a slip, step-ins, and brassiere, had been washed as well. Grubbs found one dead ant tangled in the trim of the step-ins. Of the drugs taken "from purse of deceased," he found liquid isonipercaine, or Demerol, capsules of secobarbital sodium, and a yellow amphetamine tablet.

There was no other reporting about the findings of any examination of Annie Jean's body, beyond the one reference to "pictures of the body of Mrs. Barnes." The report, again, led to more questions than answers: Why would evidential clothing have been washed? And what kind of "white uniform"? From all that we'd heard, Annie Jean worked as a secretary. We needed to ask Ralph if he remembered what his mother was wearing that Friday night.

And then finally, in February 2005, in conjunction with a trip to a conference in north Alabama, Captain Taylor agreed to meet with us. In the follow-up emails and phone calls leading up to the event scheduled for the 11th and 12th, I said we could meet midday on that Friday on our way to the conference, or Sunday morning afterward on our return. He told me he'd call me Thursday, closer to the actual time, when he'd be able to say with some certainty when would be best.

When he called me that evening, he said Sunday was better for him. "About what time?" he asked.

"Late morning, noon," I offered. The site of the conference was about three hours north of Montgomery.

"Good," he said. "We can meet at an office downtown, where it'll be quiet, with a conference room so we can spread out." He said to give him a call Sunday morning when we were half an hour outside of Montgomery, and he'd direct us to a rendezvous location.

Sunday, February 13, was clear, cool, and breezy. We drove south on Highway 21 from Jacksonville, skirting Mt. Cheaha, and the Talladega National Forest. Somewhere south of Sylacauga we called Taylor on his cell phone.

"Stay on 21 south. It becomes 231," he told me. "Where 231 ends take a right and that will bring you into downtown. Go left on Washington, I believe, and that leads right to the capital. We'll meet in front of the marble staircase at about 12:15. I'll be in a white Ford pick-up with a camper shell. What are you driving?"

But 231 didn't end, it merged with route 80 and we found ourselves headed across the interstate and into south Montgomery.

"Damnit," I said, once it was clear we were off track, loosing a little frustration, frustration from finally being so close and yet, seemingly, derailed, or worse, again. I just didn't understand reluctance for its own sake. And if it was reluctance with cause, why? No good answers came to mind.

But the capital was easy enough to find once we turned around, though we wound up on the back side of the building and drove all the way around it until we saw the idling pick-up near the capital steps, just a few minutes late.

"Trouble?" he asked, through his opened window.

"No, other than unfamiliar territory."

"Follow me," he said, and led us back up Monroe, past the Crampton Bowl, and into the parking lot of the Alabama Peace Officers' Association building. Corporal Taylor was finishing up a phone call when we got out of the car and stood waiting outside, the wind buffeting our hair, and notes.

"Pete Taylor," he said, extending his hand after he emerged from his truck. Into his seventies, Pete's six-foot-plus frame is a little stooped, and he walks with a slight limp from an aching back. He is otherwise fit looking, balding, and has energetic blue eyes behind thick, wire-rimmed bifocals.

At the door he fumbled with a couple of keys trying to find the right one. "My fingers don't work so well anymore," he explained.

Inside, he turned on lights, and led us through the rooms, past a kitchen, into an office space, to the conference room. He looked at the long table, then turned around, saying, "I don't know about you, but I've got to find an ashtray."

Back in the kitchen, pulling a glass ashtray from the cabinet, he opened the refrigerator door and said, "Help yourself to a drink," waving at shelves of Coke, Diet Coke, Diet Dr. Pepper, Sprite, Miller High-Life, and water. He pulled out a Sprite. Suzanne and I chose bottles of spring water.

Framed certificates hung on the walls over the office desks, in between shelves of bound documents and complementary hand-outs, calendars, pencils, notepads, and brochures. On a side table sat a bowl of candy, as if in preparation for trick-or-treaters: bite-sized Snickers, Milky Ways, and peppermint discs. The conference room is adorned with photographs of over seventy years' worth of association presidents. "You hang around long enough, they'll make you president," Taylor said. I found his picture in a lower row, 2000-2001 past president.

"So you're interested in the Annie Jean Barnes case," he said, sitting at the head of the table. We sat in armchairs to his left. He opened his Sprite and pulled some medication out of a breast pocket, lining the pills up on the glass-topped table. "Everyone wants to write a book about cases I covered, it seems." He told us about a brother-in-law, "a successful attorney here in town," who's writing about another of his cases.

"Annie Jean Barnes, though, to quote Doc Rehling," he said, who was the director of the state toxicology lab at the time, "was an unusual and interesting case."

He finished taking his medicine and lit up a cigarette, exhaled a plume of smoke, sitting back in his chair, head angled up, rubbing at his chin. He crossed his long legs out from under the table, turned slightly toward us, said, "It's too bad, but I just destroyed all my field notes on that case not too long ago. I kept everything for years, and finally just ran out of room. We didn't have computers back then. I suppose I could have had everything micro-fiched, or saved electronically somehow. But who's got the time for that?"

I couldn't quite believe my ears, and I was pretty sure that a seasoned investigator would catch my reaction.

He turned to Suzanne and said, "I finally started reading your book. At my age it takes some effort to read anything. I'm lucky if I can get through my motorcycle magazines. I guess I'm about a third through it. Not what I expected, but it's interesting. What kind of book are you going to write about the Barnes case?"

"Non-fiction," Suzanne told him.

"The truth," he said, slowly nodding, raising his eyes toward the ceiling. "There was a lot of talk about a cover-up with that case. I was first called into the case when she was still in the hospital. It's common practice for the local authorities to call in state investigators to do the field work. That way, the local guys,

Scotty Byrne in this case, have nothing to lose, and they can take all the credit." He paused then, and asked, "Have you talked to the family?"

"Some of them."

"And do they know what you're doing? They agree?"

"Oh yeah," we told him. "You might say they're anxious to see what we can find out."

"I just want to be sure of that before I say anything. I wouldn't want anything that comes out to cause them any more pain, or embarrassment."

He hemmed and hawed a little more, then said, "What about Scotty?"

"We're told he won't talk."

A knowing grin flashed across his face. "That doesn't surprise me." And then it disappeared. He held his mouth crooked, "like a long-time tobacco chewer," Suzanne later said.

"Scotty and I go way back," he said. "In fact, when that became common knowledge, Chief Jones sent two other investigators down to Brewton to take some of the heat off me," he said, and chuckled. "But Scotty knows everybody. You can't go anywhere in this state and not find someone who knows Scotty Byrne. I mean, he knows everybody."

And everybody knows him, we'd already heard several times, from self-professed friends and detractors alike. Though none of them, it seems, can induce him to talk.

Taylor suddenly got up from the table. "With my back, I have to stand up every now and then, just to keep it working." He stretched himself upright and hobbled into the office space, returning with white association tablets for each of us, "In case you want to take some notes," and a fist full of candy that he spread out over the table top. He selected a mint from the offerings, slowly unwrapped it, and continued.

"I guess it was that Friday night before she died that I visited Annie Jean's hospital room. She had a brother in there with her. What was his name?"

"Windham. Buddy Windham."
"Right," he said. "She was recovering. Everybody said so. Doc Strandell said so. She was still pretty doped up when I tried to talk to her, drifting in and out. So I explained to her brother that I had some other business to tend to, that I'd be back in a couple of days, when she could talk. But then she died."

He took a few languid drags off his cigarette before squashing it out.

"When I came back to Brewton, the town was in an uproar, the press speculating all kinds of wild theories, and they wouldn't let it go. When they found out about my association with Scotty, that's when they started talking about cover-up, and pay-offs. And that's when the office sent Dickson and Hanson down. We sat up that entire first night and I told them everything I'd been able to find out so far. A week later, after they'd looked into the matter on their own, they came to the exact same conclusion: that we weren't dealing with a homicide at all."

"You're saying she died of natural causes?"

"No, no. That was what Doc Shoffeitt first said, but that was an unfortunate choice of terms. I'm saying that a beating didn't lead to her death. She did suggest to me that Doc Perry had beaten her, yes, but that's not what killed her. We knew he was seeing her, and that he probably abused her just as he did his wife. What Shoffeitt meant to say was, there was any number of natural explanations for her death." He started enumerating them for us. "They found a blood clot in her heart," pulling back one long finger, "She could have died from general deterioration from her drug addiction, and I think there were some complications with either her liver or kidneys, too, most likely from the drugs."

"What about the cigarette burns, and the sexual abuse?"

"That was Doc Strandell who spread those stories. You know what he said to me? He said, 'They must have sold tickets to her.' But Shoffeitt reported that she was on her menstrual cycle at the time, and that explained all the blood. We never found any evidence of foreign objects being inserted." He reached for another cigarette. "There was no evidence of that. There was evidence she'd recently had intercourse, but that could have been any time. And the cigarette burns?" he said, lighting up, "Fire ant bites. Shoffeitt said it looked like she'd been lying on an ant bed. And sure enough, when we went back out to the camp, we found a huge ant bed with an indentation on it, looked like that's exactly what happened.

"The perception was that a lot of shenanigans went on at those hunting and fishing camps, and I never doubted those old boys didn't do a lot of drinking and card playing and carrying on out there. But we never could place anyone else out there at the cabin that weekend. None. Doc Perry wasn't even in town at the crucial time. He was in Pensacola. Dickson and Hanson confirmed that."

"Doing what?"

He rubbed at his chin some more, said, "I don't remember what. Business, I suppose, though I never knew what kind of doctor he was. Everybody just called him Doc. I don't even know if he had an M.D. Was he an optometrist, maybe?"

"No, just a general practitioner," Suzanne said. "Rosemore was the optometrist."

"That's right, Rosemore." He thought about that for a moment. "Here's what I think happened. I think she went out there, gave herself those injections, got doped up, drunk, stumbled around the place, fell numerous times, and finally passed out on that ant bed. That's what I think happened, but nobody wanted to believe us. I remember the chief of police, Chief Holt, Glen Holt, he was running against Scotty for sheriff at the time, campaigning that if he was sheriff, he'd get to the bottom of things, getting the press and everyone else riled up.

"I remember telling him, I said, 'Chief, your badge is as big as a sheriff's. If you think there's something to clear up, what's stopping you?' Well, that ticked him off. I didn't know him that well at the time. I'd only been in the territory since April. Took a long time to mend that fence, but we did, became good friends, till the day he died."

"What about the drugs?" I asked. "That investigation."

"We were investigating drugs in Brewton before she died."

"Involving Perry?"

"No. Now it's probably true that he got Annie Jean addicted, and his wife, too, but that's not what we were investigating. Illegal, certainly, but that's not what we were investigating. We were looking into an alleged narcotics ring.

"It's funny, but most places think their drug problem is worse than it really is, and that's what we found in Brewton. Sure, there were a couple of marijuana fields, and some kids selling powdered sugar out of the college bars as speed, but we didn't find any racket."

"What about insurance?" Suzanne asked.

"Insurance?"

"Is there a way to find out if she had any life insurance?"

"I don't know about that. And I don't remember if we ever asked that. That's usually one of the first things we ask, but I don't think we did in this case. I don't remember why not."

"She may not have been the type to have life insurance," Suzanne offered.

"No, no, she wasn't," he readily agreed, and repeated, "But that's usually one of the first things we think about. We've got two state troopers in prison for murder right now, and that's how we caught them. Insurance.

"One of them, Joe Duncan, killed his girlfriend Elizabeth, another state trooper, for insurance. She was my secretary for years, and when she told me she was going to take the trooper's exam, I told her that was a bad idea. 'You'll pass the test, all right,' I told her, 'but I don't think you're cut out to be a trooper.' I didn't think she was tough enough. That may have just been the chauvinist in me. Times were different back then, you know. Turns out I was right. She took the test, passed it, became a trooper right here in the Montgomery area. She met up with Duncan, who was a real scumbag. He was married, but he said he loved her, was going to leave his wife and marry Elizabeth. They took out policies on themselves, naming each other as beneficiaries, and then he canceled his two days later. He called her one night when he was off duty and she was on, wanted to meet her out of town. She drives up to this deserted place, he walks up to the car and shoots her dead, then goes off down the road to a bar.

"Nobody can raise her on the radio, so we start searching for her from the last spot she was known to be. Joe joins in on the search, saying he hadn't heard from her all night, but starts off in the opposite direction from where we found her squad car, her body still inside.

"When we find out about the insurance policies, start looking at him as a suspect, he changes his story, says yes, he was supposed to meet her that night, but she was already dead when he got there, said he was so upset he went out and got drunk."

"We asked him, 'But Joe, why did you walk in the opposite direction if you knew where the car was?'

"'I didn't want you to suspect I'd done it,' he said. Dumb. There's nobody dumber than a criminal. It's just stupid to think you can get away with a crime. He never confessed to killing Elizabeth, but we got him.

"We had a big, national case here, I remember. Henry Lee Lucas, the only death row inmate in Texas to have his sentence commuted from execution to life without parole. They want to keep him alive, thinking there may be more murders he can tell us about. He killed Ann Gilmore, the wife of the warden at Draper, right near here. Kidnapped her in town, took her out I-65, killed her, left her body tied to a tree with the seat belt out of her red Cougar, drove off." He sat there shaking his head. "For some reason people have a habit of dumping bodies along I-65. We're all the time finding bodies along a stretch by Evergreen, Georgiana. Henry Lee was a bad man. Turns out he'd killed people all across the country. His partner told us a story about how once they were riding along in a stolen car, picked up a hitchhiker. One minute Henry Lee's riding along playing with the hitchhiker's dick, and in the next minute he slits his throat, cuts off his dick, and dumps the body. Then he just rides along for miles and miles, gnawing on that poor guy's severed dick. A crazy, bad man.

"Know how we knew he killed Mrs. Gilmore? Because he slipped, told us what color the seat belt was. It was red. We never released that detail. That's how it's done, you hold back a bit of information only the criminal would know. But there's nothing like that in the Barnes case."

"Then why'd they call the grand jury?" I asked.

"SOP," he said simply. "Anything else I can tell you? Have you seen the official investigative report, the coroner's?"

"No, not yet."

"Tell you what I'll do. I'll make some phone calls, see if I can get you those records."

"That'd be great."

"Who knows. You could do all the investigating possible and still not have all the answers. Or you might stumble upon something we missed. You never know," he said, standing up, retrieving the ashtray, leftover candy. "You sure the family approves of what you're doing?"

"Ralph said he'd be willing to have his mother's body exhumed, if that's what it takes," Suzanne said.

"D-N-A," he said slowly. "We didn't even know what that was back in those days. We never thought to save tissue samples or body fluids."

We gathered up our notes, water, helped Taylor shut the place back down. Outside, standing near his truck, we thanked him for his time. He said, "Good luck to you. I'll make those phone calls."

"We'll be in touch," I told him.

"I hope you find something, I really do. There are questions that haven't been answered. They deserve to find out what happened, if you can find it." Then he asked, "Which way are you going back?"

"65 south," I told him.

"Do you know where your turn is?"

"I think so."

"Follow me. There's a left turn down a few blocks. I'll point to it as we go by."

We got back in the van, started it up, and while we were waiting for Taylor to turn his truck around, asked each other, "What do you think?"

"I really liked him," Suzanne said. "It would have been a lot easier to believe there'd been a cover-up if he hadn't been so nice, if he'd been more like a bad-ass cop, you know."

"I think he's cagey, at best. I mean, why the hell would he destroy his field notes, knowing we've been asking about the case for a year and a half?" I asked, not really looking for an answer so much as venting.

We turned left off of Pelham onto Monroe again, down capital hill. "I wonder," Suzanne started as we rolled through the deserted Sunday afternoon downtown. "How he didn't know what kind of doctor Perry was. I remember a woman at one of my readings, whose mother was one of Perry's nurses, saying her mother had gone to work one day after Annie Jean died and the office was closed, police cars all over the place."

"And?"

"Well, if they visited his office, and interrogated him, how could he not know the kind of medicine he practiced?"

"Good question," I said. "Here's some more: What about Perry's alibi at the 'crucial time,' when they never could pinpoint the exact cause of death? And that blood clot?"

"What?"

"Well, it's just a hunch, but if she'd been bitten by ants so severely that they looked like cigarette burns, she would have been full of venom, you know, which, I think, is a natural anticoagulant."

We slowed for a red light. I studied the stickers on the back of Taylor's truck: Fraternal Order of Police. Alabama Peace Officers' Association. National Rifle Association, associations, every one of them, whose prime motive is to protect their own, and as such, an association which meant Taylor, at least in part, was just another good ol' boy.

A motorcycle cop rolled up in the opposite direction, stopped for the light. It turned green, and as they passed each other in the intersection, Taylor waved to him, he nodded back.

At the next light he signaled that as our turn, waved, and continued west on Monroe.

"Didn't he say he thought Annie Jean stumbled around inside, then passed out on the ant bed, outside the cabin?" Suzanne asked.

"Yeah."

"Think about that report we saw: one sheet was soaked with urine, which sounds to me like she passed out inside. And another sheet had blood stains, and grass stains."

"That's right."

"Like she'd been outside, and then in the bedroom, not the other way around."

"There's something else about what he told us Shoffeitt said: 'All that blood.' Like there was a lot of it. 'All that blood.' The toxicologist's report only mentioned a couple of spots, remember?"

"Right."

"Pete sure wanted to insist there'd been no foreign objects inserted," I went on.

"More than once."

I thought about that a minute, said, "It's kind of like an investigation in reverse."

"What do you mean?"

"Well, he answered so many questions we never asked."

"Right," she said. "And I wonder why he got Perry mixed up with Rosemore. He was a neighbor of ours, a real character. One of the few Jewish families in town. I used to go to synagogue in Pensacola on Saturday with his daughter, and she would go to the Methodist church on Sunday with me."

"And he was an optometrist?"

"His office was in that same block where Willie's restaurant is, which used to be a pharmacy, run by Jimmy Atkisson, who was a good friend of Rosemore's, and I'm told he knows a lot about it, is willing to talk."

"Knows a lot about it because he was there?"

"Oh, hell," she said, half laughing. "You could spend a lifetime trying to unravel who was actually there and who was rumored to have been out there. I could list twenty names for you, starting at the very top of town. I think that's what bugged me so much about it. I mean, I'm a kid, right, but sitting in church after all that came out, I'm looking around and there's a name, there's a name, there's a name. Who do you look up to? Who do you believe?"

"Care to name those names?" I tried.

"Wouldn't be right," she said, "without confirmation," then laughed again. "My mother said the morning after Annie Jean was brought in to the hospital that housewives all up and down our street were calling each other and visiting in their yards and beside their clotheslines, asking each other, 'Was your husband there? Was yours?' It's going to be messy untangling the rumors, if it can even be done, with so many of them dead now."

"We need to find a way to get Scotty Byrne to talk."

"Yeah. Here's an irony for you. My grandfather was also a longtime sheriff over in Worth County, Georgia. He knew Scotty, took him quail hunting in south Georgia, thought a lot of him, thought the world of him."

"No kidding."

"Yeah. But I don't think it will get me an 'in' with Scotty."

"Was Holt on the list?"

She looked at me sideways. "I doubt it. Why?"

"Just wondering what he was so hopped up about."

"I'm not sure how trustworthy he would have been. You know the Davidson case, out by the White Horse? Plenty of folks think Holt was mixed up in it somehow, that it had something to do with drugs, or drug money."

"Thought you didn't have a drug problem in Brewton?"

"This was the 70s. By then cocaine and pot were everywhere. You would have thought, though, that where there's money, there're drugs. It sure surprised me to hear Pete say they found no problem in '66."

"Yeah. Right. Do you know that the same grand jury that heard Annie Jean's case handed out fifty-one other indictments, most of them drug related?"

"More than a couple of marijuana fields and peddling bogus speed? Curious, don't you think?"

"The place is crawling with curiosities."

"But do you think there's enough for a story?"

"Oh, yeah," I said. "Absolutely," which turned out to be a rather poor choice of words. There would be nothing absolute about our investigation, especially Taylor's pledge to help us get the official reports.

Murder Creek

"Like a Fiction Novel…"

…WAS THE HEADLINE of the op-ed column in the October 20, 1966, Brewton Standard. In this editorial, Gardner saved most of his concern for "the good name of Brewton." This would be his last commentary on the case only three weeks after calling for an "investigation to rid this community of so much that is undesirable." Despite the public support for that editorial stance, what appears to be most undesirable is any comparison to Phenix City, a few hours to the north, and east. While there is no debating the legitimacy of such a concern—in fact, a book published eleven years earlier was entitled, Phenix City: The Wickedest City in America[31]—what about Annie Jean? Still lecturing its readers against unfounded speculation, rumor, and gossip, the paper stated that much of the story being so readily circulated through town was made up from the kind of stuff that could "only happen in a novel of fiction." The most immediate issue amongst the public after the story broke was not any contention about what had happened, but who was involved. As Suzanne said, the talk in the street, the main topic in discussions at the market, or in church, across neighboring fences or over clotheslines was not about disputing the deed itself, but rather: "Was your husband out there?"

What happened, one has to wonder, between September 29, when the stance was one of literally giving voice to the "sheer amazement that this could happen here" shared by most of the populace (in an editorial headlined, "Our Failings, Our Shame, Our Obligation") and the October 20th dismissal of the story as only so much fiction. What could account for such a disconnect between the Fourth Estate* and its constituency? What happened to the professed obligation? There's probably no divining what might have occurred behind the scenes at this point, but the "report" issued just days earlier—Dr. Shoffeitt's verbal "natural causes" determination—gave rise to continued speculation rather than resolution.

It was an unusual shift. The determination was delivered to Henderson, Byrne, and Taylor the week before in a hastily called, late-night meeting in Mobile—not Brewton, not Montgomery, and not Auburn, where the forensics department was headquartered. Pearson, with the Birmingham News, citing how "highly unusual" it was that a verbal report was issued at all, tried for a month to get something more official, something documented, some kind of explanation out of the investigators or the DA. Why, he asked, if the cause of Annie Jean's death was natural, couldn't they release details of the investigation? Or why couldn't they say exactly which natural cause they were referring to? Nelson Grubbs, the toxicologist actually working the case wouldn't answer, other than to say it wasn't his job to determine what the natural cause was, beyond probing whether there was an unnatural cause of death, a criminal cause.

Upon convening on November 14, it became the Grand Jury's task to decide if there were any chargeable offenses committed in the case, this "mysterious," and unexpected death from "natural causes." Because they didn't find any, didn't return any indictments, that testimony was sealed. All that's readily available of those proceedings is the published report, and the reported characterization of the proceedings from Dr. Strandell, who couldn't "believe they're getting away with this," while he is also

---

* Dating back to Revolutionary times, the "Fourth" – after the nobles, the clergy, and the commoners – Estate is, according to Edmund Burke, "more important than them all" to the survival of a democracy.

said to have claimed that "you'll never know how much money was spent" to make the story go away.

But that information came from the victim's family, thirty-seven years after the fact, long after Strandell, and Perry, and Henderson, and Shoffeitt had died. Even if the information was relayed by more than one family member, independent of each other, it's not much to go on, which begs the question, as Suzanne put it, "What's the story?"

We weren't, to be honest, when we examined what little information we had at the time, entirely sure that we had a story. And when I wrote it all up—the result of which was more or less what you, reader, have read so far—and showed it to an acquaintance who's been in the publishing business for decades, in various capacities, everything from editor to agent, he was skeptical as well. "What's the pay-off, the take-away that will compel book-buyers to invest $25 and 15 hours of their lives in this book? To be convinced that racism, class-ism, elitism, corruption still exists in the Deep South? That this is yet another example of the rottenness at the core of deep-southern society? Why, of all the murders, do we need to hear Annie Jean's story, especially given that Suzanne has already written a fictional account?

"Indeed," he continued, "isn't this story better served in fiction? Isn't that the best way to get at and reveal the truth?"[32] an eerie correlative of Gardner's editorial stance, or worse.

The exchange also reminded me, uncomfortably, of a comment I'd seen in a Mississippi newspaper during the uproar over Emmett Till's murder, back in the summer of 1955, the year Phenix City was declared "the wickedest city in America." Fourteen-year-old Emmett Till, you may recall, lived in Chicago and was down in Money, Mississippi, visiting family, when he was abducted by a white mob, tortured, lynched, and tossed in the river. When the body was found and returned to Chicago, it was only through his mother's insistence on an open casket during the funeral proceedings—unflinchingly displaying her son's battered and bloated body—and photographs of the body subsequently published in a September, 1955, issue of Jet magazine, that the "rottenness at the core" of deep-Southern society's racism became a serious, and prominent issue. The question of "How could this happen in America?" while the rest of us were luxuriating in those laconic Eisenhower years, became an imperative that demanded answers, and action.

Some locals, though, didn't quite get the force of the imperative, didn't quite understand all the hullabaloo. One local who shrugged it off as so much status quo, was quoted as saying, "the Tallahatchee's full of niggers." So what's the problem?

The problem is, the imperative's still pertinent: How could this happen? The problem is, Annie Jean's children, whose lives didn't have the best of prospects to begin with, have been damaged, if not ruined, by not knowing, still not knowing, forty years later now, exactly what happened, much less how. One inescapable conclusion is that if you're poor, and relatively insignificant, you are, if need be, disposable. In a society where money begets power, and power begets privilege, and privilege begets entitlement, and entitlement, too often, begets impunity, anything could happen, and does. Is this news? No. But then, neither was Emmett Till's body washing up on the riverbank, at least not in Mississippi.

Is it a story worth telling, though? That seems to me more or less moot. Because the story itself refuses not to be told. Because it is not, per se, a story about corruption in the Deep South. Or that "racism, class-ism, elitism," still exists there. It is a story, rather, about what can happen when those things are constitutionally granted sway over subjugated classes or races, what happens to the fundamental principle of the rule of law, what happens to the entire notion of Democracy. If there is any relevance to the axiom that "as the South goes, so goes the nation," or any pertinence to the question, "What if the South had won the war?" then yes, the story of Annie Jean Barnes is worth telling, because the case of Annie Jean is an example of what the result would be if such speculation was truer than we'd like to think, because Brewton, in the 1960s at least, was the model embodiment of that reality.

The framers of the 1901 Alabama Constitution crafted a document that reflected their attitude that—Appomattox be damned—the South had won the war, and it wasn't until the 60s that the federal government succeeded in putting a dent in that attitude and reigning in its rogue, or quaint, definition of representative government. Even George Wallace met his match in the 1901 Constitution. He could defy the U.S. Constitution and the Supreme Court and keep Alabama's public schools segregated for a generation after the Brown decision, but he couldn't wield enough strong-armed currency to alter the state's term limits.[*] Despite all of that national attention, Wallace's political shenanigans, his defiance of the Brown edict, that Court's long-overdue decision outlawing the state's poll tax, even speculation that Wallace's infamous schoolhouse doorway grandstanding had been a completely staged event (at the same time the Birmingham News was reporting on the Barnes case, they revealed that there were actual marks where Wallace was to take his ridiculous "stance" for "segregation forever!"), the story of the

---

[*] He could, and did, flex those muscles in other, more devious ways: In 1966 he put his wife, Lurleen, up as his gubernatorial successor after he failed to amend the constitution's term limits. Then, most notably, of the 14 senators who blocked the amendment, every single one of them either decided not to run for reelection, were defeated, or, in one case, committed suicide.

"mysterious" death of "relatively unknown" Annie Jean Barnes came, and went.

As such, we decided to start over, to go to primary sources, the root of the story. We went back to Brewton.

Murder Creek

Alco Redux

AT THE VERY least, if we accepted the proposition that there were people who had information but wouldn't talk about it, we weren't serving the story very well. So we planned to ask. "Even if they say no," which is what we expected, "that's still part of the story," I reasoned, and set about determining who was still alive, where they were, and getting their addresses.

We went by Joyce's house again, because one person we needed to talk to, needed to get to talk, was her Aunt Willie Mae. No one was home, so we left a note and then went on to an old friend of Suzanne's who would know who was still in Brewton, who might have information about the case, etc.

He gave us a bunch of names, many we'd heard before, how they might be connected, where they were. Then he said, "You know George Jr.'s back in town, don't you?" He meant Doc Perry's son.

"No."

"Yup. He buried his mama last December, and is still living in her house. I don't know why. There's nothing for him in Brewton. Settling her affairs, I suppose."

"Will he talk to us?"

"I doubt it."

"Is there anybody that will?"

"You can try. Is Skeeter still around? Hugh Caffey's down in Florida. Peggy Owens is still alive. She might know something. She was Doc Perry's nurse for a while. And Billy Joe Griffin, wasn't he the hospital administrator at the time? Grover Smith, of course, is the sheriff now, and was Holt's deputy then. And James Taylor, he'd be a good one. He was Scotty's deputy."

"What about Scotty?"

"He definitely won't talk. He might, actually, blow your head off."

We waited for him to laugh, but he didn't.

"Why all this silence?" I asked later.

"It's a small town."

"Yeah, I understand that. But if there's really nothing to talk about, if there are no dark, dirty secrets to the story, why do we keep hearing that the people who could actually confirm that, won't, refuse to?"

"Good question."

"Why did Jr. even come to your reading, if there's nothing to the story?"

"And why is he back in Brewton?"

"Why is that so strange?"

"Well, there really is nothing in Brewton for him."

"Tell me more. What do you know about him?"

According to what Suzanne had heard, George had no family left in Brewton, and very little, if any, family anywhere. His only sibling, sister Susan, had died in 1999. As both his parents were only children, he would have distant, far-flung cousins, at best. His father had grown up in tiny Geneva, Alabama, and his mother, Marguerite Perry, nee Johnson, had moved to Brewton from Auburn, by herself, a young woman looking for work, just before World War II.

On a scholarship to Harvard, George left Brewton right out of high school, in 1966. Susan left a couple of years after that, once she'd graduated, marrying and moving away, against her parent's wishes, we were told, though that's difficult to confirm. Not a lot of people remember much about the family, because George Sr. and Marguerite were not a very sociable couple, didn't belong to any of the churches or civic organizations, didn't have many friends. They were, by all accounts, a troubled—his drinking and philandering, her drug addiction—but intensely private family. A story goes that once Jr. got away to college, in the midst of the civil rights and anti-war movements, that his father threatened to kill him for his liberal politics, though a family acquaintance we did talk to didn't remember that.

Junior taught for a while around Cambridge after graduating Harvard, then went on to Harvard law. He practiced in Houston for a few years, and then Atlanta—worlds beyond Brewton, Alabama. During those early years in practice, the mid-70s, we were told George drew up divorce papers for his parents several times, but Marguerite never signed them until 1976, when the couple finally split. By then, Doctor Perry was at the nadir of a downward spiral into drug and alcohol abuse, before dying alone. Laid up in the house on Bellville emptied by Marguerite after the divorce, he couldn't even take care of basic bodily functions during his wasted final months, relying on others to happen by and clean him up. At his funeral, we were told, "maybe 10" people showed up.

"Speculation," I said, of the thirty-year-old statistic. "All we've got is speculation and rumors. Maybe Gardner had it right after all, way back when."

"You wouldn't think that if you'd been here at the time."

"We need to talk to George."

"How are you going to do that?"

"I'll just write him a letter. Ask."

That was one aspect of all these peripheral discussions that was increasingly troublesome, that assumptive leap that Perry and Byrne and the rest wouldn't talk. Has anyone asked them? I kept wondering.

So I did. I wrote him a short note when we got home from Brewton, told him who I was, what we were doing, and why. I said we'd be back in Brewton in ten days, and we'd like to meet. He didn't have to talk about anything he didn't want to. "I'd be interested in your take on the curious legal proceedings of the case, if nothing else," I wrote.

A week later, a Tuesday evening, he called. "This is George Perry. I just got your letter today." He explained that he didn't always stay at his mother's house, the address we'd gotten out of the phone book, so he was a little late getting the mail.

"But you are back in Brewton?"

"Most of the time."

"And would you be willing to meet?"

"Sure. When will you be here?"

"This weekend," I told him. We were scheduled for an event in Monroeville that Thursday, Friday, and Saturday morning, planned to drive to Brewton that afternoon.

"How about lunch, on Sunday. Say, twelve-thirty or so. Do you know the Mexican restaurant, by the old Winn-Dixie?"

I did. We agreed on all counts. I thanked him, hung up, and spent a few surprised moments pondering the complete lack of resistance from someone who reportedly "didn't want to talk about it."

The next surprise came twenty-four hours later, when Joyce called. Yes, she would be willing to meet again, and would be home that Saturday evening.

The final surprise in the set occurred Friday evening, in Monroeville, where we chanced to meet Mary Tucker that same afternoon: an email from Pete Taylor. While I try not to put too much reliance on such things, such sets of occurrences, Taylor's note was more than a little curious. That fact that I heard from him at all, number one. It had been months. After repeated attempts to follow up on his offer to make some phone calls, to help us obtain some of the official documents from the case, I had yet to hear back from him—a span of time that had stretched to over a year—until that Friday in Monroeville, on the eve of our returning to Brewton to start the interviewing process all over again.

But the content of his message was even more curious than its unexpected arrival: he didn't say anything about his efforts toward locating any of the old documents, which, if he was responding to the nine month old email, would have been what I'd asked about. He did say he'd be willing to meet again, but then added that he just didn't know how much of a story there was to tell. "I just don't think it was a homicide," he said.

"In my opinion the case lends itself much better to the nucleus for an excellent fictional novel," especially, he said, if we utilized what he called our "political license in your writing."

He went on to note "some questionable actions" by "some officials," sex, drugs, wild parties, "but no homicide."

Not that the thought hadn't crossed my mind, especially with all the far-flung hints being lobbed at me. Between the agent, the editor, and the investigator, I take three to constitute a quorum: What if, say, some down-and-out detective, slogging his way through another boring domestic surveillance case—which is ninety-percent of his load, as it is for most PI's, actually—whiling his time at some late night coffee shop or Waffle House, and he picks up a tattered paperback copy of In A Temple of Trees, someone had left behind. Now with all the idle time on his hands, endlessly staking out apartment complexes or cheap motels, he's not adverse to spending that time reading newspapers cover-to-cover—especially if it's an out-of-town gig—even doing the crossword, and crypt-o-quip puzzles, or flipping through an occasioned novel, especially crime or mystery novels, where he can read about all the stuff he fantasizes about but never gets to do. Now something about the blurb on the back cover, saying the novel was "inspired" by an actual event, or something about the inscription scrawled on the title page to the original owner, or even wondering about a particular dog-eared page within the book gets his curiosity bubbling and he starts to wonder about that actual event, feeling himself drawn into the forty-year-old case, investigating a case everyone had thought was gone for good, and no one wants to talk about. Usually, in books like that, there's no end to the line-up of bit actors willing—hell, eager—to tell their version of events. This guy doesn't have that luxury. He has to rely on the characters from Suzanne's novel, who are somehow conjured up by his stirring about and make cameo appearances throughout the book, prodding him along.[*]

I even thought up a name for this guy, but didn't go any farther than that, as that would have been off the point, which made me wonder all the more why Taylor would've nudged me in that direction. Maybe he's got aspirations of his own along those lines, in his retirement. I didn't know, but planned to ask. It'd be a lot easier, I'll grant. A fictional rendering would, at the very least, assure us of an ending. That's the thing about fiction. However tortuous the arc, you can count on an ending. We had no such expectations in this case.

---

[*] I thought that aspect, conjuring Hudson's characters, particularly appealing: People still say of Railroad Bill, Brewton's famous 19th century Robin Hood character, that he conjured himself into animals and such to escape the law.

I answered that, yes, we would be interested in talking again, that we were still pursuing the story. But first, we wanted to hear what Joyce, and most importantly, George, had to say.

Joyce was alone in the house on Franklin Street when we arrived. She told us that she had called her brothers and sisters, advised them we were coming and invited them, but no one had showed. She seemed more disturbed by that than by us.

I told her we mostly wanted to keep her informed of our progress, that we were trying, again, to get to people who didn't want to talk. "We've had some success contacting people, telling them exactly what we're doing, and straight out asking if they'll talk to us. We thought we'd try that with your aunt, if you don't mind."

"I don't mind, but I doubt she'll talk."

"Do you have an address?"

After trying to recite it but not being sure of the house number, she went looking for a phone book for verification, saying as she searched, "It's right around the corner almost. Just past the college, take a left at the church." Then, flipping through the pages, she said, "Why don't I just try to call her?" and dialed the number.

Joyce turned from the phone after the brief conversation, said, "We can go over there right now, if you want."

We were stunned.

We all got in the car and made the two-minute trip to Willie Mae's. It was a small house, with a little fenced yard at the end of Fleming Road. The fence and yard were already festooned with flags and red-white-and-blue bunting, all set for 4th of July, still two months away.

"At least she's taken down her Easter decorations," Joyce said, indicating that her aunt's house was made up to commemorate one occasion or another almost constantly throughout the year.

At the screened front door that led into a tiny living room, Joyce called through to Willie Mae sitting in an easy chair fronting a television set. "Come on in," she answered, not moving. We filed in and took seats, as she waved around. Joyce sat on a couch against the far wall, me on a stool in front of Willie Mae, and Suzanne in a ladder-back chair just inside the door. It backed up to a set of curio shelving packed with do-dads and trinkets, figurines and plates. The whole room was jam packed with such keepsakes—on every and all available horizontal or wall space—but, Suzanne said later, "No dust anywhere."

Willie Mae sat there watching us, not interrupting her dinner of fish sticks and milk, in a housecoat and slippers, looking none too pleased to see us. Finally, between bites, she asked, "What do you all want to talk about?"

"Well," I started, "this is Suzanne Hudson," but didn't get any further before Willie Mae pounced.

"I know who you are," she turned and sneered, with all the indignation of one of the Pentecostal preachers to be found on the other side of the creek that she grew up listening to and cowering before. It's a feature of East Brewton that some attribute to its depressed class status, the abundance of storefront churches—evangelical, Pentecostal, Church of God, Nazarene, Community of Christ—that can be found on virtually any corner throughout town. "I know you," Willie Mae repeated. "That book is wrong, awful."

She pivoted a little in her chair to more fully face Suzanne. "You were wrong to write that book. That's not my sister. Annie Jean was a good person. She worked hard all her life. She would never do anything like what you wrote about."

I could feel Suzanne buckling under the contempt.

"She had a hard life, caring for those children."

"Tell me about that," I said, finally finding an opening. And, just like that, her tirade seemed defused, for the moment.

Suzanne said later that she'd wanted to get down on her knees before the woman, eye to eye, wanted to tell her, "Your sister's death haunted me," but didn't, she said, certain that she would have set to bawling.

Willie Mae talked about Fred, how he couldn't hold a job, but that Annie Jean followed him around the country, trusted him, "Dragging those babies this way and that." How when she finally left him after his arrest in Texas, the family rallied around her. "It's a good family," she insisted.

"Did you grow up in East Brewton?"

"No." Her early years were spent moving from turpentine camp to turpentine camp, mostly in an adjacent county, Monroe. She remembered that two older stepbrothers rode her on the plow-stock, when she was still a baby, as they worked the company fields. It was the Alger Sullivan Company then, and would later be absorbed into T. R. Miller through marriage.* When the motion put her to sleep, they would lay her down beneath a shade tree.

Being the first daughter, "I was babied until I was ten years old," she said. Annie Jean was three years younger. "My daddy rocked me to sleep every night until I got too old, and tipped the rocker over," she said, and laughed.

---

* "Timber marries timber," I was told: the south Alabama equivalent of old world dynastic perpetuation.

Her father found work in Mobile's shipyards once the war cranked up, but was hurt there in 1945. That's when they settled in East Brewton.

Annie Jean followed in their father's footsteps, leaving home in 1954, after graduating W.S. Neal High School, moving to Mobile looking for work. Her graduation came a year later than it should have, after she missed part of the 1953 school term with Ralph's birth. That's where she met Fred.

"Were they ever married?" Joyce asked.

Married?" Willie Mae answered, taken aback by the question. "She took his name."

"I know that. But I don't remember them ever divorcing, so I wondered if they were ever married."

"Of course they were," her aunt said, but didn't offer anything like a date or a location, or any other suggestion of proof. "You can probably look it up in Mobile, if you want to." Then she leveled some of her disdain for Fred. "Whenever Annie Jean and Fred and the kids were staying here between moves, you couldn't leave any money around. He'd steal it." And when Annie Jean left himin 1962, divorce or no, "It was the best thing she could've done."

After Annie Jean'd brought them back from Texas, "she worked as a secretary for Ed Leigh McMillan," Joyce said, proudly. I later found out the source for that pride. Ed Leigh was one of the biggest of the "rich dogs," as they're referred to in Brewton.

"I don't remember that," Willie Mae said.

"Then why would he give her all that help?"

"All what help?" I asked, but aunt and niece were at it.

"You don't know," Willie Mae charged.

"I want to know, Aunt Willie."

"You don't know."

"She was my mother. I want to know."

"She was my baby sister!" Willie Mae said, near tears, before her anger surfaced again.

It was hard, is still hard, to reconcile that blend of hurt and anger and grief and defensive fury and fear when pressed by certain questions, or aspects of the story, certain, unpredictable aspects.

"You don't know," she repeated.

"That's why I'm asking," Joyce relented.

"I found her," Willie Mae said, turning back to all of us.

Willie Mae and Lucille, Annie Jean's best friend—the two worked weekends together at the White Horse—had gone out to the camp that Sunday morning.

"And he was out there."

"Who?" I asked.

"Scotty Byrne."

"Why?"

This was the moment, I knew, the moment Brenda and Joyce had warned about, where Willie usually clammed up, or got angry. She fiddled with her tray for a moment.

"He just wanted to watch, I guess."

"Watch? Watch what?"

She looked up at me, said, "He smiled at us, said to Jean, 'What happened to you?'"

"What did your sister say?"

"Nothing to him. He knew what happened to her."

"What did she say to you?"

"Nothing."

"Nothing at all?"

"Aunt Willie?" Joyce broke in. "I thought you knew who beat her, who was out there."

"I do know."

"Then why don't you tell us?"

Again, she paused. She started to reach for the milk, then withdrew her hand. "Because I can't."

"Was it Scotty?" I asked outright.

"No. I can't," she answered, not entirely convincing or direct.

"Granny always talked about Inez Sowell," Joyce tried.

"Shut up!" Willie Mae snapped. "You don't know."

"Well, I think I have a right to know; she was my mother."

"You don't have any right! You don't know!" And they were back at that perplexing stalemate.

"Who is Inez Sowell?"

"Was," she corrected. "Nobody."

"She worked with Marguerite, didn't she?" Joyce offered, but Willie Mae wouldn't budge.

I could feel the interview unraveling, the room closing in, all of the stacked bookcases and hanging trinkets threatening to bury us all. "What about in the hospital? You were there when she..."

"No," she cut me off. "She died all alone. No one was there."

"But?" Out of the corner of my eye I saw Suzanne glance toward the door, as if checking to be sure it was still there.

"Aunt Willie?"

"No one was there."

Joyce shrugged.

"And the Grand Jury?" I tried.

"They wouldn't let us testify," Willie said, closer to tears now than fury.

"But we were there," Joyce said.

"Not inside," she recouped and snapped again. "It was fixed. Doc Strandell, he came out, said, 'You'll never know how much money...' It was all fixed. We had to go see Governor Wallace to get them to investigate."

"You went to Montgomery?"

"Scotty and them wouldn't do nothing. And then Perry's brother-in-law did the autopsy in Auburn... All fixed, right down to the insurance."

"Perry's brother-in-law?" I stopped writing at that point, dizzied by the emotional fluctuation.

"Marguerite's brother."

"Are you sure?"

"Yes, I'm sure."

"What about the insurance?"

"They wouldn't pay off the policy. We never saw any of that money."

"We got a little," Joyce said.

"A thousand dollars each," Willie Mae sneered.

I asked Joyce, "Where'd that come from?"

"Who knows."

"Shut up!" Willie said.

I sat back in the chair, not sure what to do. I had unconsciously scooted up to the edge of the seat, trying to understand what was happening. "Did you ever talk to Doc Perry about all this?"

"He wasn't there."

"At the camp?"

"No. He was in Birmingham."

"Birmingham?"

"Yes. Visiting his sister."

"His sister?"

"Yes," she said, clearly getting annoyed by this point. "His sister."

We'd been there over an hour already, and it was clear we'd just about worn out what welcome there'd been. There were so many other questions I wanted to ask, but didn't sense any real willingness to continue on her part and didn't want to jeopardize the possibility of a return. I thanked her for her time, apologized if we'd upset her, and asked if it'd be all right if we visited her again some time.

Surprisingly, she consented, then asked, "What are you going to do with all this?" "Well, we're working on a book about your sister's death."

"A book?"

"Yeah, we'll let the family know when it gets near pub-date," I started, but then, as if mentioning any book at all cued her to return to the topic she most wanted to cover, as if it were the real reason she'd allowed us to come over and everything else had only been an interlude, she turned to Suzanne and said, "I object to that book," repeating, "You were wrong to write that book," even as we were standing, readying to leave.

"I'm sorry if it bothered you," Suzanne allowed.

"Bothered me right away, first three pages. I had to put it down. Just wrong."

"Thanks Aunt Willie," Joyce said, stepping between them. "I'll call you soon."

Willie Mae's anger turned instantly to hospitality, as she reached for Joyce's hand, said, "All right, dear."

We all shook hands, thanked her. She even said, "It was nice to meet you," and again suggested she'd be willing to talk again. Then we bid her goodnight, the dizziness morphing into a headache.

In the car, Joyce said, "See what I mean? She gets mad."

"Sorry," I offered.

"Oh, it's all right. She'll get over it. I just don't understand, don't understand why she won't tell us."

"What about your uncles?" Suzanne asked.

"They don't talk to each other at all, Aunt Willie and her brothers. Big fight when Granny died," she said. "My sister Jenny, she don't live here, but she kept a bunch of the papers from then. Maybe she could help you."

"That'd be great."

We chatted some more the rest of the ride back to Franklin. She hinted at other, darker disturbances in the family, repetitive disturbances experts like to claim are the results of unyielding poverty and hopelessness. An ambivalence started to set in, standing there at Joyce's doorway, about how much comfort she could derive from the truth of her mother's death, if there is such a thing to be found, seeing that faraway look in her eyes, as if she's irretrievably removed from the days when traversing the rutted dirt driveway was a joy-ride, getting stuck on the railroad tracks an adventure, or a shiny new pay-day quarter all she ever wanted.

Before shifting gears to reverse out of the driveway, I asked Suzanne, "You still want to spend the night?" It was already almost nine.

She looked at me, fear palpable in her eyes. Instead of declining—which I know she wanted to—she said, "What about tomorrow?"

"True," I said, and dropped it from park. To break the silence I asked, "I thought both Doc and Mrs. Perry were only children?"

"That's what we were told."

"Well, we can sure find out if Marguerite was related to any of the coroner's staff."

"She would have known that, Willie Mae."

"Maybe it's just memory corroded by rumor."

"And anger."

"You all right?" I asked.

"So angry," she repeated, as if stuck.

"At everyone, it seems," I tried.

She knew what I was doing, but let it go. "Doesn't make sense. How can you tell a child she doesn't deserve to know about her mother's death."

"As if the kids' grief doesn't count."

"Only hers. Isn't natural."

"But is it explainable?"

"I'm almost afraid to ask that," Suzanne said.

Murder Creek

The Colonial Manor Inn

THE COLONIAL WAS made famous by "A Love Song for Bobby Long," the title track of the 2004 Travolta movie, written and performed by Grayson Capps, the son of Everett Capps, a former East Brewton resident.[*] "Brewton, Alabama, at the Colonial Inn…" the song begins. Bobby Long was an infamous Brewton derelict, a charming, proselytizing, alcoholic intellectual. The one segment of the society that moved with relative ease back and forth across Murder Creek, according to the elder Capps, was the derelicts: "Brewton's derelicts mingled freely with East Brewton's," he said. Bobby Long was found dead in the woods near the Colonial not long before the new millennium, a victim of his own habits. He would have fit right in on the commemorative list at the end of Philip K. Dick's A Scanner Darkly, the former acquaintances, Dick wrote, who "made only one mistake" in life: their addictions.

The Colonial Manor Inn remains a headquarters for Brewton's addictions, drugs, and prostitution, just south of town. Next door is a Day's Inn, which is where we stopped that Saturday night. A sign on the door announced that as of June 1st, they would no longer accept patronage from locals, from anyone within a thirty-mile radius. Barely passing that test, we went in and asked for a room. They were booked up that weekend though. Habitat for Humanity was in town, had taken over the place. They were building two new homes there at the time.

"Is there anywhere else?" we asked.

---

[*] And the screenplay for the movie was adapted from Everett's book, *Off Magazine Street*.

"Just the Colonial. Other than that, you have to go thirty miles south to Atmore, or thirty miles north, to Evergreen."

As we were turning to leave I asked, "What's with the sign?" meaning the prohibition of locals.

"We don't want to end up like the Colonial," was the answer, answer enough to try and find someplace else to stay.

The lack of hotel rooms was a far cry from 1925, when the Chamber brochure boasted of not just "the finest hotel between Montgomery and Mobile," but three other hotels as well, all for a population one-twentieth of the current citizenry. There were five hotels in Brewton back in the 1880s, remember. We ended up crashing the night at Ronnie Tucker's, another of Suzanne's former neighbors and high school acquaintances.

Ronnie and Debbie Tucker live in a rustic ranch house on a few acres of wooded land not far from the White Horse, down a side road off 31, near the turn for where Perry's camp house was. They remembered the Barnes case well and were more than willing to discuss it. And both of them are tangentially connected to the case in odd, but interesting ways.

Debbie, for a time growing up, was a neighbor of the Barnes'. Her former sister-in-law is married to Grover Smith, current sheriff. Debbie's ex-husband was Timothy Baber, murdered in 1979. She's seen and experienced all of the unsavory aspects of the Barnes case, and is the one who said, "If you want someone killed," Brewton's your place.

Ronnie is a forester who knows most of the timber lords. "Rich dogs," he called them. He was first married to "King" David Miller's granddaughter, a stratospheric circle of Brewton's society he may have only had access to, a theory goes, because his step-dad at the time was Skeeter Huxford, one of the "dogs," though that hadn't insulated Ronnie from more than his share of pain and death over the intervening thirty years.

Murder Creek

I went to sleep that night in their guest bedroom thinking about those circles as overlapping worlds and all the gravitational and repellent forces governing them, how they seemed to collide and recoil but never really break completely free of each other's orbits. I wondered about Debbie crossing the creek, or Ronnie's trajectory, and how they both seemed to have landed comfortably enough in their spacious home. Not that they haven't suffered any cosmic retribution for their movements. Quite the contrary. I was just thinking in terms of comparison to Annie Jean, who may have died for hers.

The next morning we left well before our scheduled lunch time. We wanted to tour East Brewton some more, wanted to see the streets Joyce had mentioned, the Neal spread north of town, another place the Windhams had lived and worked for a time.

In 1962, Michael Harrington wrote, "The poor are increasingly slipping out of the very experience and consciousness of the nation."[33] He was talking about the effects the urban renewal and suburban flight of the 50s and 60s had on this country's poor, how that was creating a new, more insidious cloak of invisibility shielding them from the middle-class and the affluent. When the shanties and tenements were torn down and replaced by high-rise apartment complexes, it only served to drive the poor deeper into the cracks, out of sight, and out of mind. The tidy parks along Snowden Road, on the bank of Murder Creek, and off St. Nicholas Avenue, fronting the main square over in Brewton, are prime examples: gone are the dilapidated shacks and infested apartments where cardboard boxes served as cribs and shoes were a luxury, despite Harrington's claim that "America has the best dressed poverty the world has ever known,"[34] except they're not really gone, just no longer visible. The result of that is the poor become "politically invisible" as well: "It is one of the cruelest ironies of social life in advanced countries that the dispossessed at the bottom of society are unable to speak for themselves. ... As a group, they are atomized. They have no face; they have no voice."[35]

It's a condition particularly aggravated by Alabama's constitution, where "home rule," the very thing southern states' rights advocates went to battle for, local control by county commissions, is suffocated by constitutional requirements for legislative bills and state-wide referenda before any action can be taken. If the poor are invisible to the local citizens as they come and go in their daily routine, they are non-existent in the hallowed halls of the legislature up on the Hill in Montgomery. That a woman should turn up beaten and left for dead, subsequently die and disappear, is not shocking within a construct that rendered her invisible, disappeared, long before she went to that camp house that Friday night. The construct is shocking, or at least it should be.

Other former residences of the Windhams' and the Barnes', the trailer on Gillis Avenue, or out along Ridge Road by the Neal spread, had been sanitized, too, all part of East Brewton's acclaimed "Vision, Growth, Progress." The only evidence of growth on that Sunday morning seemed to be centered around, or determined by, all the competing churches throughout East Brewton. What kind of vision or progress the aggregate congregations provided is debatable. The sign out in front of the First Community Church declared, "I don't know why people change churches. It makes no difference which one you don't attend."

Spying the paucity of cars in the parking lot, I commented, "Pretty thin crowd."

"Maybe the message is a swipe," Suzanne said.

We decided then to go on to Jalisco's, the Mexican restaurant, get a table and wait for George Perry Jr., still well before the appointed time.

"The church people will start flooding the place any minute now," Suzanne warned.

We got there just before the sky opened up and a brief spring storm drenched the parking lot. We watched diners dash from their cars to the covered sidewalk outside the place, where they paused and shook off the water before entering.

"What's he look like?" I asked, after a while, fearful of missing George in the steady stream of patrons.

"I don't really know."

The next fifteen, twenty minutes was a game of trying to guess the most likely suspect. We knew only that he was almost sixty years old, which wasn't much help, and that he'd probably be alone. That distinction was some help, as we looked for lone diners amongst the family clusters, dressed out in their Sunday finest. We watched one, then another solitary man enter, stand in the threshold surveying the room, and then move briskly to a table in the interior. Finally, he came in, dressed more casually, slight build, short-cropped, light, thinning hair, glasses, looking around more tentatively, like someone who didn't know what they were looking for, as opposed to the others. He took a few cautious steps along the partitioning that separated the smoking from the non-smoking section. I stood and said through the lattice, "George?"

"Yes," he said, and came around to our side. "How did you know?"

"Took a chance," I told him as we shook hands. "That, and you answered to George."

"Of course."

"This is Suzanne Hudson."

He greeted her, sat. The waiter was at the table immediately. We'd been stalling for half an hour, promising that we were waiting for someone.

George declined the menu, said, "I know what I want," then asked about another waiter, his regular waiter, we found out.

"He's not here."

"How is he," George asked, with a level of concern we didn't understand at the moment.

"They had their baby."

"Wonderful." George placed his order, then said, "If you see him, tell him George said congratulations."

Then he filled us in some. "Great guy. When I come in, he helps me with my Spanish. He's been laying low for a while, though."

"Why?" I asked.

George looked over the top of his glasses at me, as he unrolled his napkin, set out knife, fork. He turned to Suzanne. "You grew up in Brewton? Went to Miller?"

"Yeah," she said. "Graduated in '71."

They chitchatted some more, tossing names back and forth, looking for common acquaintances or experiences. Five years separated them. In terms of teen-aged years, high-school years, especially, that's a life time, so it wasn't a complete surprise that their particular lives had never intersected. Still, it was another indicator of how insulated some of the layers of the town could be, one from another, even in a small town like Brewton. It was a treat watching the exchange, the revisited memories, George's animation. "He's exquisitely likeable," Suzanne said later, "and interesting." She said she'd love to talk with him about a lot of things.

"I left right after graduating," he explained, "in '66," when Suzanne would have been not quite thirteen. "And pretty much stayed away for over thirty years. Didn't you hate it here? The obscene exploitation, the sense of entitlement the elites have?" he asked.

"I never saw much of that."

"How could you miss it?" he chided her, gently, then shifted, opening up. "I'll tell you when my politics changed." I thought he was going to tell his version of the story we'd heard about his father threatening him, after he'd gone to Harvard. But it was earlier than that, considerably earlier.

"I was thirteen," he said, which would have been '61. "I was visiting a cousin who was interning that summer up in D.C." Kennedy's first year as president. "When I came home, Willie Stanley, dad's driver, picked me up at the airport in Montgomery. He always did that, sent Willie, never picked me up himself. Anyway, we're driving back, and there's this great barbecue place south of Montgomery, so I suggested we get some lunch. We stop, get out of the car, I say, 'Come on.' Willie stands there, speechless, looking a little confused, before telling me, 'I can't, Mr. George.'" George grew animated telling the story. "I'd been up in Washington, right, I'd seen whites and blacks out together, dining together, and didn't really think anything about it. I was thirteen," he stressed. "It was as if I'd just that moment realized the kind of world I'd grown up in, and hated it. I went in the restaurant, bought a couple of sandwiches; we ate together in the car. Changed me forever. I remember trying to talk to my dad about it," he said, as our food arrived. "But he wouldn't listen, wouldn't even listen. I don't think we ever agreed on anything again," he added, with a distant look in his eyes, as we lowered ours.

"So," he started, after fidgeting with his plates, setting foil-wrapped tortillas aside, positioning his iced-tea. "The Barnes woman."

"Right."

"You're writing a book?"

"Right," I said again.

"I wasn't here, you know. Don't have any first-hand knowledge, and so don't know how much I can tell you."

"We're just trying to find out anything we can. For her children, mostly. They've never been told much."

"That's the kind of entitlement I'm talking about," he said, leveling a fork at us. "That they think they can get away with something like that."

"We're still trying to figure out who."

He studied me, said, "Most of what I have to say will be off the record," sounding every bit the lawyer he was. "I'll tell you when it's not. Tell me what you do know, first. Have you seen the ABI report?"

"Not all of it. Not most of it. Just the forensics stuff. But we did talk to the lead ABI investigator, Pete Taylor."

"What did he tell you?"

"Well," I started, "he said he was called into the case that Friday, after Annie Jean's sister found her at your father's cabin, and she'd been in the hospital all week."

"Wait a minute, wait a minute," he stopped me, leaning over the table. "You really think she was still alive when they found her at the cabin?"

Suzanne and I looked at each other. I didn't know how to answer that. Suddenly aware of the ambient noise all around us, I wondered about the volume of our voices. "Everything we've seen and heard so far says that," I tried. "Taylor, the children, the newspaper articles: They all say she died in the hospital."

He didn't seem fazed at all by my evidence. "I was in Cambridge, remember. So all I know is what I heard at the time. But there are at least a couple of conversations I had later that led me to believe she was dead when they found her."

How could that be? I remember thinking, but don't know if I actually asked yet.

"My sister Susan called me after it happened," he said, holding up one finger.

"When?"

"I don't really remember exactly when, but she was all upset, saying, 'A woman's been murdered at the camp house.'"

"And?"

"Some years later, 2000, maybe, I was having a conversation with my mother about it, and in the midst of it I said something like, 'Mother, a woman was found dead at our camp!' to which she responded, 'No, she died in the hospital.'" By this point he was halfway out of his seat, bracing himself on the tabletop, leaning well into our space, glaring adamantly. "I said to her, 'How do you know?' She didn't respond. I'd put the same question to you, now," he said, relaxing back into his chair. "You need to look at that ABI report."

We looked at each other again, the question flushing both our faces: How do we know?

"Go on," George said, poking at his chicken.

I continued to recite Taylor's version of events, his departure, return, the flap over his familiarity with Byrne, Dickson and Hanson being called in, their confirmation of his assertion that

119

Annie Jean was alone at the camp, how they never could place anyone else out there, that George's father was out of town—

He shook his head, clearly agitated by what I was saying. "Wait a minute," he stopped me again. "They're saying he wasn't there?"

Again, I had that feeling like someone had pulled my chair out from under me, had to regain something like balance, before saying, "We've heard two different stories, that he was either in Pensacola, on business."

"What kind of business?"

"Didn't say, or ask, apparently."

"Or?"

"Or in Birmingham, visiting his sister."

"My father didn't have a sister."

I shook my head then. "You're saying he was there?"

"I know he was. I'd testify to that."

If there had been food in my mouth at the time, it would have fallen out.

He pushed his plate away with something like disgust. "Look, I'll tell you a little story, and this one you can use. Now every conversation I had with Willie about it made me think my father was there, and that she died at the camp, and I trusted Willie, had a very good relationship with him." Willie Stanley, the driver from back in '61, had been the family aide. He was the one, we were told, who picked Annie Jean up that Friday night. "But then, about the time I was getting ready to go to graduate school, June of 1970, my dad took me shopping for a car, down to Pensacola. I don't remember if it was on the way there or back, but we got into a discussion about Annie Jean, and he said to me, 'I sure needed Willie's help that night.' And then made a reference to the 'body.'" George paused, shaking his head, looking like he was going to retch from the memory. "That upset me so much, I stopped the car and got out, started walking down the highway. I didn't know which direction I was going, just that I wanted to get away from him, wanted to distance myself from him and that awful story as far and as quickly as I could. I know he was there," George repeated, taking one last look at the remains on his plate before giving up on it, shrouding it with his napkin.

"Jesus," I said.

He looked up at me. "Anything else?"

"Only about a million little questions."

He smiled at the reference, then said again, "You need to get that ABI report."

"What I'd like to get is the Grand Jury testimony."

"Have you asked?"

"Not yet."

"Don't know if I can help you with that one," he said, though didn't say he couldn't help, curiously.

The sun was in full furnace by the time we finished, baking the asphalt, steam rising from the remnants of the earlier storm. Our glasses fogged immediately, and we all stood there outside Jalisco, temporarily impaired, wiping them clear, before thanking George again, Suzanne hugging him, saying, "Come down to Fairhope sometime, come visit," and then parting.

Murder Creek

How could that be?

THE TRAFFIC, ONCE out of Brewton's limits, was sparse that Sunday afternoon, which was fortunate, as the scenarios played out in my head.

"How is it possible that she might've been dead at the camp but not pronounced until six days later?" I asked, letting one out.

"It's not possible. Can't be. There's no way they could have pulled that off."

"No way?"

"Is there?"

I didn't really want to loose that theory, didn't want to be sidetracked into a path of trying to prove something versus attempting only to discover, or uncover, whatever was there. I'm a fairly decided proponent of the notion that you find what you're looking for rather than what's really there, more often than not. "There's a way."

"How?"

"We don't know nearly enough to piece that puzzle together, but it's a huge question now, isn't it? I mean, what other way is there to begin to explain the discrepancy between George's and Pete's stories?"

"Maybe George is nuts."

"Right." I was pretty sure he wasn't nuts, at all. He seemed like a very nice guy, though clearly pained by that part of his history.

"Then how?"

"Ask this first: who's told us they saw her alive in the hospital?"

"Taylor. And Willie Mae."

"Right. And weren't we uncomfortable about her anger, that defensive anger?"

"That's not much."

"No. But she was either completely mistaken about Perry's sister and Marguerite's brother, or she lied."

"She could easily be mistaken. Explain Taylor."

"I don't know. Why would he tell us Doc was out of town—and not just say it, but give us this elaborate story about Dickson and Hanson 'confirming' he was in Pensacola—when George is certain, is willing to testify, otherwise?"

"Error?"

"Pretty critical error, don't you think?"

"You're saying he lied?"

"Or was lied to, if what George said is true."

"Maybe he's nuts," she said again.

My head started hurting from it all. Almost home, as we rolled around the square in Bay Minette, the courthouse cordoned off, under renovation, I was looking forward to a cold beer. "I'm trying to remember," I said, rubbing at the dull ache, "did Pete say he saw Annie Jean, or just that he talked to her brother—because she was still too doped up—and told him he'd be back?"

"You've got notes, right?"

"Yeah," I said, and then added before I could stop myself. "Or maybe he's gaming us."

"Gaming us? What do you mean?"

"What if, a retired, life-long lawman, in failing health, with a sick wife, he's got no real thrills in a life that was filled with them, is 'lucky' if he can get through his motorcycle magazines, and a couple of knucklehead writers come along asking about a forty-year-old case, and he decides he's going to have a little fun with them."

"That sounds like fiction. You don't really think that, do you?"

"No, not really. But it seems like we have to rethink everything, that it'd be our mistake not to consider anything within the realm of possibility."

"What about the newspaper reports?"

"Reporters report, they write what they're told."

"Doc Strandell?"

I just looked at her.

"No, no, no," she said, waving me off. "We heard he was one of the good guys, trying to look out for the family. Remember?"

"Yeah. Who told us that?"

"This is nuts."

"Did Joyce or Ralph ever say they saw their mother up close, still alive, when she was brought home?" I asked.

"No. Just the opposite. They were shooed out of the room."

"Right. And they weren't allowed to see her in the hospital."

"When she was supposedly recovering."

"If they were that close, how could they have kept her from seeing them?"

"It's not like kids couldn't go in there," Suzanne said. "I remember going there any time I wanted to, walking in and out without any problem. We used to play in the hallways, for God's sake."

"Did you remember a morgue, somewhere to keep a body for six days?"

"You're not serious?" she said. "Oh, come on. This is crazy! Why would they keep the body six days before declaring her dead? And how?"

It was easier to formulate an answer to the former, if it were true: "Maybe the number of days is inconsequential, beyond that's how long it took state investigators to show up." As to how, the prospects of what it would have taken to manage such a thing were bewildering, and frightening. "Think of who would've been involved."

"How could that be?" Suzanne asked again, and again.

I thought of that line, "isn't this story better served in fiction," and as tempting as the suggestion was, I thought, "No, it isn't." There didn't seem to be anything but fiction swirling about the story, forty years of fictions, and the story hasn't been very well served at all. A retreat into fiction would have been an abandonment of the story, and Annie Jean's children. The only thing that would serve the story well was fact and, hopefully, truth.

We needed the ABI report—George's voice ringing in my head—but would have to get it without Taylor's involvement. Even though determined to resist what amounted to, at the moment, merely vague implications, that didn't mean I was going to ignore an insistent skepticism. I would go to Montgomery and try to get it myself.

A day or so later, while I was still planning and prepping that itinerary, Suzanne told me she'd gotten a call from Willie Mae's daughter, Linda. "She said she didn't want us visiting her mother anymore. Apparently we upset her too much."

"What?"

"That's what she said."

"Was she nice about it?"

"Oh yeah. Very pleasant. Had all kinds of nice things to say about Annie Jean, too. Said Annie Jean was the first adult to treat her like her feelings really mattered, how if she laughed, you couldn't help but laugh with her. Linda grew up in Mobile, but remembered trips to Brewton to visit her granny—said granny was a saint—and that she always had someone to play with there. Said: 'I cherish those times even though I had to sleep in between those twins and one of them always had their feet stuck up in my face.' She talked about Annie Jean loading them all up and taking them to the creek. Said, 'I loved to hang clothes with her'."

"Nice."

"Nothing but. Didn't want to talk about Annie Jean's death, though. Other murders, Timmy Baber's, the Kirkland girl, but not Annie Jean's. 'Scotty Byrne knows,' she said, if we want to talk to someone, 'but won't ever tell'."

"That again. That's it?"

"No, we chitchatted some more about her family, etc."

"How'd she get your number?"

"I don't know."

We had lunch with Wayne Greenhaw. He and his wife Sally were readying to go back to Mexico, where they spend half the year. Wayne, along with Donnie Williams, had just recently won one of the state's biggest literary awards for The Thunder of Angels, the definitive story of the Montgomery bus boycott fifty years earlier. Wayne had been a budding newspaperman at the time in Tuscaloosa and later moved on to Montgomery where he was a reporter for a number of years, as well as the author of sixteen other books of fiction and nonfiction. Wayne is a sly and gracious gentleman, into his sixties, quick to laugh, always open to conversation, as good a listener as he is a storyteller. He told several stories of his time as a beat investigative reporter for the Alabama Journal during the 50s and 60s. He said he and a partner, a black radio DJ, were always twenty-four hours ahead of state investigators on cases. "Got so they would follow us around to get the story," he said, and chuckled.

You can still learn a lot from following Wayne around. Hell, you can learn a lot from just noticing what he notices: he has a habit of looking sideways at the world, catching what's on the periphery, the stuff most the rest of us miss, which is one reason we wanted to spend some time with him.

We told him the Annie Jean story. He'd read Suzanne's book, but didn't remember ever hearing anything about the Barnes case at the time, though he did know many of the actors involved, Taylor, Scotty. "Was Doc Rehling in on it?" he asked.

"Yeah. As the Director of Forensics, he would have signed off on the report. Pete quoted him as saying it had been 'an unusual and interesting case'."

Wayne chuckled, low, and shot me one of those tangential, knowing glances out of the corner of his eye, from behind his thick glasses. "He was a real bastard," he said, though smiling when he did so. "I was working a story once, in the sixties," he started, in his slow, methodical drawl. "A young black man was pulled over by a cop north of here, beaten, and taken to jail. The next morning they found him dead on the floor of his cell. The police tried to say he fell out of his bunk and cracked his skull. Doc Rehling testified that upon examination," shifting his voice, his posture, "the deceased had 'the thinnest skull he'd ever seen,'" shaking his head at the memory, one among many, it seemed, of such memories.

We told him some more of the story, what we were lacking, trying to get. He gave me the name of the reference librarian at

Murder Creek

the state archives, Norwood Kerr, said, "Mention my name. He'll help you out." Wayne made a point of acknowledging the assistance of Kerr, and the rest of the staff and volunteer librarians at the archives, in the writing of Thunder of Angels, deservedly.

Norwood told me that the archives wouldn't have ABI reports or Grand Jury proceedings. I'd need to go directly to the Department of Public Safety for the former, the Escambia County Courthouse for the other. He gave me a name and number for a Captain Arrington with the ABI. A call there initiated what would be a long, tentative process of obtaining the report. Likewise with the courthouse, as they turfed me from office to office.

An email exchange with Forensics turned up two additional reports in the Barnes case. They required a formal request and fee for each. Rather than squander the time it would take to send mail back and forth, I decided to submit the requests and fees personally, to the AFDS offices in Auburn, an hour or so east of Montgomery, since I was headed that way anyway.

Inside the little foyer of their building on Wire Road, I was surprised—though maybe shouldn't have been—to see a shrine to Doctor Rehling, side-by-side in a display case full of heritage drug paraphernalia—pipes, bongs, clips, rolling papers. There was his badge, congressional proclamations, and a formal portrait of the former director. The photo was clearly dated, could easily have been forty years old. In it, he's wearing a dark brown federal suit over long-sleeved white shirt and thin necktie; black, plastic framed glasses looked like 60s vintage. Dark hair shaved close around the sides of his head, the tuft on top Brill-creamed to hold its flip. I couldn't look at the image without thinking about Wayne, the story he'd told us only recently.

Murder Creek

The clerk came back through the locked door into the holding area, said yes, they had the records I'd requested. She took the fees, said it'd be two, three weeks.

Inside the first-floor reference room of the Alabama Department of Archives and History there was a trove of articles, diaries, photographs and transcripts, originals and/or preserved copies. In the micro-fiche collection I found nineteenth-century editions of the Brewton Blade, whose editor had instigated the whole "cat fight" imbroglio over the Escambia County seat. A subscription to the Blade cost a dollar a year in the 1880s. What was most interesting was the content, as I scrolled through edition after edition. At the top left corner of the front page they published a poem each week and then followed that with a short story, presumably fiction, before printing anything that could be taken as news over in the right hand columns, announcements, mostly, about the travels of its citizens, events in town, visitors.

On my third trip there, one Thursday afternoon, I was hunkered down at one of the long wooden tables flipping through The History of Escambia County when a stout, middle-aged, athletic-looking man I'd noticed roaming the stacks came up to the table. "I see you're researching Escambia County," he said. "I'm from Brewton," tapping his chest and then extending that hand. "Buddy Mitchell."

"I know you," I said, shaking his hand. "The bridge," the one that spans Murder Creek.

"The people's bridge," he stressed, and laughed. "What are you working on?"

I gave him an abridged version of the story, which he vaguely remembered, mostly for the uproar it caused at the time. He said he'd be willing to talk about it sometime, but didn't know how much help he'd be. He did say that he'd gone to school with

George Jr., and Scotty Byrne's son, Chip. He gave me a phone number and turned toward the exit. Then he stopped and said, "You might try the Atmore paper. They were a little bigger than the Standard then, might have given the story more coverage."

I'd been through the Birmingham, Brewton, and Mobile papers on previous visits and they all carried comparable articles on the event over the month it was news. It had seemed, up to that point, that Pearson, with the Birmingham News, was the most dogged journalist working the story, but I filled out a request for the 1966 film of the Atmore Advance.

When the librarian delivered the box of film from the storage room, the spool that I needed hadn't been rewound, so when I threaded it into the reader the print was backwards, and upside down. I looked at the clock ticking toward closing time, thinking about the three hour trip back to Fairhope, and just about called it quits for the day. One of those internal voices, a voice born of more of that latent frustration with our lack of progress, or the lack of cooperation, or maybe just the strain of reading the print, was saying, "Hell with it." I mean, it wasn't that we didn't know who to go to or what questions to ask, as much as those questions just kept getting deflected. Typically, I thought, you follow a line of inquiry until it yields pertinent information or dead-ends. We kept getting detoured, denied, or ignored. Then a volunteer passed by.

"This film is backwards," I told him, without thinking. I don't know if it was just a silly response to the tension, but I almost chuckled at how emblematic the words sounded.

"Ah, some folks, when they use the old machines," he said, pointing off to a corner of the room, "they get the reels mixed up. Here," he said, spinning the reader around. "Try that."

"Thanks," I told him, a little sheepishly, as the print came into view, though in reverse chronological order.

Murder Creek

I didn't find anything new until the October 13th edition. A front page article headlined, "Autopsy Reveals Woman Died of Natural Causes," reported Shoffeitt's verbal report of the day before. But then, in the last couple of paragraphs of the column, I found this:

Dr. George Perry, Escambia County Coroner, told a Montgomery Advertiser reporter late Wednesday afternoon that he did not know what Mrs. Barnes was doing in his cabin. He told the Advertiser, "I took her home about 5 a.m. Friday and was sitting there talking to her mother when she left in a taxi."

He continued, "I found her when I went to my cabin Sunday morning. When I found her, she was not injured in any way. She was just drunk on something. She had been to my cabin before, but I do not know what she was doing there Sunday," he told the Advertiser. (p. 1)

I read it again, and then a third time. Perry was the coroner? Perry saw her that Sunday morning, in the cabin?

"How could that be?" I mumbled to myself, staring at the black-and-white proof that George wasn't nuts, that at least one of his claims was true, not to mention the revelation that Perry was the coroner at the time, and that Taylor's version of Annie Jean getting doped up, stumbling around and then passing out on the ant bed couldn't possibly reconcile with Perry's quote.

I rewound the film in a hurry, gathered up my stuff, thanked the good librarians again, and was out the door, into the blistering afternoon heat, and on the telephone as soon as I reached the interstate, I-65, southbound.

More Questions

"HOW COULD TAYLOR not know?" I asked Suzanne into the phone. "And again, offering that off-the-wall suggestion that he didn't know if he was a real doctor, an MD doctor, everybody just called him doc... We didn't ask anything about that."

"True."

"We have to confirm if he was the coroner, one way or another."

"I'll ask Gene."

If Perry was the coroner, there's no way Taylor didn't know that. In fact, there would had to have been some discussion about who would perform the autopsy, which explained why Shoffeitt signed off on the report, without any reference to a medical doctor, so far as we'd seen. Obviously, there was enough of a conflict to take Perry off the autopsy, but why, I wondered, hadn't that come up before now?

Now, more than ever, we needed those reports. On each of the trips to Montgomery, I'd called the ABI offices, only to leave messages, never getting through directly. On the return trip from Montgomery, I finally got a call back. "Number Withheld," flashed up on the screen as the phone rang.

"Hello?"

"Mr. Formichella? This is Captain Lloyd Arrington, Alabama Bureau of Investigation. Tell me what it is you're looking for?"

I gave him the case numbers.

"That's an old one," he said. "I'm not sure what we'll have on that one. Why do you want it?"

"I'm working on a book about the case."

Murder Creek

"Normally, we're pretty reluctant to release files. Somebody's always coming back later, looking to sue us for breach of confidentiality or something."

"The files are classified?"

"No, nothing like that. But lots of times they do have personal information families might not like given out."

"It's the victim's family that wants me to do this."

"It is, huh? I don't know. I had a case over in Georgia, some years ago, woman was raped, murdered, family ok'd release of the file. They still sicked the lawyers on me. Tell you what," he said. "Let me do some digging around, see what we've got. I'll call you back."

When I arrived back in Fairhope, I'd received a note from Forensics. Seemed there was a fourth report on file. They'd need another $10 to release it.

Meanwhile, Gene did confirm that Perry was the county coroner.

That didn't assuage the conspiracy theories whispering in my head. No wonder the town was crying "cover-up" when Shoffeitt's verbal report came out.

The first bundle of Forensics material arrived a couple of days later, three memoranda from the Department of Toxicology and Criminal Investigation, as it was called then. One to Wiley Henderson, the DA, dated October 24, 1966, detailing Shoffeitt's findings. One to Sheriff Byrne, dated October 31, reporting toxicologist Grubbs' examination of "materials submitted." And the third, sent to State Investigator Chapman, dated December 6, the results of testing on the drugs found.[36] The last two, we'd

133

seen. The first one, Shoffeitt's "natural causes" determination, was new.

After beginning with a typically officious introduction, Shoffeitt, who wrote the memo under the department director's—Rehling's—signature, is the one who said, "This has been an unusual and interesting case." Apologizing, then, for the amount of time it has taken, Shoffeitt wrote, "We have a woman who entered the hospital Sunday, September 18, with narcotic withdrawal symptoms and with injuries to her body and extremities. The patient responded to medical treatment with excellent recovery until her sudden death at 10:20 AM, Saturday, September 24." After stating that the hospital record would show the patient's condition upon admission, he went on, "at autopsy the physical trauma, other than the bruised breast and swollen arm, must be listed as superficial skin abrasions and contusions with evidence of normal repair. The bruised right breast and swollen left arm, although more than superficial, do not account for sudden death with the possible exception of death from pulmonary embolism or some other complication resulting from these injuries. No such complications were demonstrated at the autopsy.

"In the absence of evidence to account for sudden death as due to physical trauma, and the absence of conclusive evidence to attribute death as due to drugs, we are left with an unexpected and sudden natural death." But in the next paragraph he reported that very thing, "the gross findings of a small, long, stringy clot leading from the tricuspid valve of the heart into the right ventricle and pulmonary artery": a classic pulmonary embolism. Together with the "microscopic findings of kidney damage and edema of lungs," the "clinical record of shortness of breath with sudden death," left "the most probable cause of death as due to a cardiac arrhythmia and pulmonary edema. A more specific cause has not been determined," he continued, "however the swollen arm, condition of kidneys, significance of Demerol, and idiosyncrasies of a drug addict are to be taken into consideration when accounting for the chain of events which terminated in respiratory failure and sudden death."

Shoffeitt then expanded upon the assertion Pete had repeated a year earlier: "Evidence was suggestive of sexual intercourse or, if not intercourse, that an object had been inserted," but, "there was no evidence of sexual mutilation as may have been the initial impression by those who observed menstrual blood," the "all that blood" Pete alluded to.

He concluded, "I cannot state just how this woman received the injuries to her body," leaving the answers to that question to the state and local officers: Who beat Annie Jean Barnes?

Attached was a file memo of the detailed post-mortem examination. He first listed the external injuries, two "abraded" areas of the right breast, areas "3 to 4 inches in diameter" at the crest of each hip, one on the mid-back, the top of the right shoulder, "needle punctures" on the lateral surface of the upper right arm, the swollen left arm with puncture marks, bruising, and abrasions, and several abrasions and contusions of the lower extremities, the "anterior surface of both knees," the "posterior surface of the right leg at the knee bend," a "small area of the inside surface of each leg," and both feet. All these, he said, were "suggestive of trauma inflicted several days prior to death."

The abdominal-thoracic examination revealed "tissue of the right breast" observed "as moderately hemorrhagic," but no hemorrhage or trauma within the cavities." The lungs possessed "a typical mottled, glistening outer surface," with "a settling of blood to the dependent parts." No "massive clot or embolus" excepting the "long stringy, fragmented, dark red clot" previously mentioned. The heart showed "normal size and shape, with no evidence of hypertrophy or pronounced dilatation," no noticeable sclerosis in the coronaries, an unremarkable myocardium and aorta. A small clot was located "slightly above the elbow" of the left arm, whose tissue had "a yellowish color, with appreciable edema fluid present." The kidneys, ureters, adrenals, spleen, pancreas, and liver were "not remarkable."

The laboratory examination of tissues, in a file memo, revealed "the presence of a trace of ethyl alcohol (0.06%) in the stomach contents," but no alcohol in the blood or other tissues, a "trace of Demerol" in the liver and other tissues, and "no other chemical poisons or powerful drugs were identified in the analyses."

"What does it all mean?" Suzanne asked for me.

"Wish I knew. Can't escape the appearance—to me, at least—that the evidence doesn't quite match the conclusion."

"Which?"

"Well, the clot, no clot, for one," I told her. "He said," flipping back through the pages, "her injuries, here it is, 'do not account for sudden death with the possible exception of pulmonary embolism or some other complication,' but 'no such complications were demonstrated at the autopsy,' hence a 'natural,' sudden death. But listen to this: 'The principal causes of death under this classification are usually related to one of the following: heart and aorta, respiratory, brain and meningee, digestion or urogenital organ system,' but he described all those as unremarkable. I didn't see any 'microscopic findings of kidney damage and edema of lungs,' and I'm no expert, but I'm not sure what the 'idiosyncrasies of a drug addict' are, or what evidence he found of that."

"We need an expert."

"I'll say."

"Anything else?"

"I still don't see how the Grand Jury could have found—what did they say?—'nothing was revealed which would warrant any action on the part of this body.' Never mind the apparent ambiguity of Shoffeitt's report, didn't he leave the door open for someone to be charged with that 'possible exception' line?"

"Any luck with that?" she asked.

"The Grand Jury? Not really. Just what was reported in the paper, that 'All witnesses who wished to give testimony were permitted to do so,' except the person who found her that morning, according to Willie Mae."

"I can't believe they wouldn't let her testify."

"Then why would she say that?"

"Protecting herself? Someone else?"

"Yeah," I said, "she hinted that she was afraid to name names, but if the testimony's sealed, like we keep being told, why would she go out of her way to say something so incredible, or un-credible, that you can't help but ask more questions?"

"How are we supposed to unravel all this?"

"Keep trying." And then I wondered, something we should have asked a long time ago, "Did they have a lawyer, the family?"

"I don't know."

"I'm beginning to hate that answer."

Norwood Kerr had referred me to the courthouse for the Grand Jury proceedings. At the courthouse I was told the DA's office was responsible for those records. The person at the DA's office in charge of that, Marsha, was in court the two, three days I called that number and left messages. When Marsha did call me back, she clarified that her office approved or disapproved the release of those documents, but it was the court clerk's office that actually archived them. She couldn't say if there would be any record of that proceeding at all, since it was so old, and, to her knowledge, they didn't record such things. "Was anyone indicted?" she asked.

"No."

"Well, then they'd be sealed anyway."

"That's what I'm told. I just wanted to ask."

"I can give you the name and number of the clerk, if you like."

A similar round of tag ensued with Kenneth Taylor, the court clerk, and when we finally connected, he first said the records were, "Confidential."

"But you do have them?" I asked.

"Oh yeah. We've got records that go back to the 1880s," the year they stole the seat from Pollard.

"Are there any circumstances under which those records would be available?"

"Well, let me see, let me look at the section that covers that," he said, flipping through the statutes. "Here it is, section 12.16.221," reading to me, "in the case of a pending investigation in the public interest, a DA or circuit judge may authorize the release of said documents."

I didn't know how much of an opening that provided, but it sounded like at least a little window.

Meanwhile, I hadn't heard back from Captain Arrington, and left a couple of more messages with his office, one a week, anyway, coinciding with what were now regular visits to Montgomery. A few days later I received another of those "number withheld" calls I'd learned to appreciate as being my friends at the ABI.

"This is Major Ken Hallford," the voice said, the bureau chief, the man who could, without equivocation, tell me to get lost. I told him what I was asking for, why, gave him the case numbers.

Murder Creek

"I don't know," he said. "Let me talk to the legal folks. I'll get back to you," and hung up.

That, by comparison, felt like a window easing shut, or freefalling, something more like a guillotine, slamming down on the story. And over the course of a couple of weeks, and no response, those misgivings intensified. Even messages left with Major Hallford's office couldn't penetrate the silence.

It was Captain Arrington who finally called back. "We're going to give you the files," he said, simply. Detailed the procedure: They would mail me a release form to sign, and upon the receipt of that back in their offices, they'd post the file.

It doesn't pay to be overly suspicious when you're trying to be an objective investigator, but it sure felt like they'd looked for any possible rationale to keep that file tucked away and out of sight. Persistence alone, it seemed, pried it loose. A peripheral concern, at best, I still couldn't wait to see what was in there.

I would have to learn how, of course. A week, then two went by, and no form arrived from Montgomery. On the eve of an unrelated trip to Columbus, Georgia, I was all set to call Captain Arrington again, tell him we'd be passing through Montgomery, and ask if I could just come to the office, sign the form, pick up the file in person, when the mail arrived.

Murder Creek

Courtesy, Service, Protection, since 1935

SO SAYS THE seal emblazoned on the Alabama Department of Public Safety stationary. "Enclosed is a copy of the above referenced investigation conducted by this department." They'd sent the whole file, case #20-1424. "Also enclosed is a Case Transmittal Form. Please sign this form and return in the self-addressed envelope that is enclosed. Sincerely, Major Ken Hallford."

"What's that?" Suzanne had asked when I'd arrived, pulling open the flap of the bulky yellow envelope.

"ABI file," I said, and couldn't help but grin.

The first thing we noticed on the case cover sheet was the date of request, "9-16-66," by "Brewton PD," and the "Date case opened: 9-16-66."

"That's the Friday before she was found at the camp."

"Typo?" Suzanne offered.

"Possible, I guess," I said, though I was having some difficulty imagining how.

The file was a hefty one, some seventy pages of departmental reports, witness lists, various statements, Tom Gardner's notes, and forensics reports. On all the formatted Investigative and Identification Division reports – "I&I," as the ABI was known then – the different investigators labeled the character of the case as "homicide," which Taylor disputes to this day.

The top report, dated October 31, penned by Taylor, details an interview he had that day with Dr. Strandell, who produced Annie Jean's medical record, describing her last medications and final activities in the hospital before she died. She was given "Combiotic" and "two cambala tablets" that morning. Her last

Demoral shot, "50 miligrams" was given at 5:45. She was "taking sitz bathes as part of her treatement for injuries" during her stay and had one from "8:00 A. M. to 8:30 A. M. the morning of her death." I wondered about that. I'd always thought "sitz bathes" were routine therapy for post-partum women after the trauma of childbirth. If that particular part of Annie Jean's condition could be explained by "menstrual blood" rather than "sexual mutilation as may have been the initial impression," according to Shoffeitt, why did they administer the baths?

A "Mrs. Hill," the "Director of Nursing," was also interviewed by Taylor. "It is her opinion that Jean could not walk by herself, at any time while she was confined to the hospital." After reading Dr. Strandell's recitation of Annie Jean's injuries as presented in the Emergency Room that Sunday, we knew why.

In a statement signed three weeks earlier, Dr. Strandell wrote,

I asked Mrs. Barnes what had happened to her arm. She stated she had fallen and hurt her arm. Examination of the left arm was then made. Just lifting the left arm caused the patient severe pain. The arm was badly swollen and there were numerous contusions and abrasions on the arm extending from the wrist up towards the shoulder and on the posterior aspect of the forearm was a large area which seemed to be twenty-four to thirty-six hours old, of a fairly large contusion and an abrasion which looked as if it had begun to start to heal. At this time the patient complained of more pain and she asked for some Demerol. The sheet covering the patient was then pulled back and the gown the patient had on was lifted up and there were numerous areas on her body of contusions and abrasions. The patient again asked for something for pain. The patient was then asked by me what had happened to her and she again stated that she had fallen. Mrs. Barnes was told by me that she could not have done all of this to herself by falling and I would not give her any Demerol for her pain until she told me what had happened. At this time with her mother present, one of her sisters present, and whether or not Mrs. Holland was standing near the examining table I do not remember; however, the patient stated that Dr. George Perry had beat her up at his cabin.

He then proceeded with a "general physical examination." Her head and neck were "essentially negative." Her lungs were clear. "The right breast was considerably swollen approximately twice the size of the left breast, and there was an area in the superior lateral aspect of the right breast which looked like the results of burns. The whole breast was red and inflamed and markedly tender and there was a large hematoma present in the breast." The abdomen was negative, and the "liver, spleen, and kidneys were not palpable." He described "an area of eroded skin and marked inflammatory reaction" around each iliac spine. "There were marked contusions and abrasions on the thighs and on the inner aspects of both upper thighs extending from just above the knees up to the perineum. Examination of the back showed an area of eroded skin over the sacrum and an area of inflammatory reaction around this area of approximately five inches in diameter. There were numerous needle marks present on both arms," as well as "numerous contusions and abrasions present over both arms, over the lateral chest wall, the hips, and the thighs." He again found "numerous contusions and abrasions over the lower extremities extending from just below the knees to the ankles," and "punched out areas similar to burns" on her feet. Annie Jean was admitted to the hospital, he concluded, "at approximately 4 P.M."

"I guess that puts to rest George's other theory," I said.

"That she died at the cabin?"

"Yeah."

"Still," Suzanne said, a look of horror on her face from the description. "You know what that description sounds like."

"The meaning behind Strandell's 'they must have sold tickets'?"

"Exactly. Question is, who's 'they'?"

Though the doctor's testimony seemed to put to rest that other question: Who beat Annie Jean Barnes? Further into the file, Taylor reported that at "approximately 3:00 P. M." on Friday the 23rd, "I went to the McMillan Hospital along with Buddy Windham and talked to the victim. After about a fifteen minute conversation I talked to her mother Mrs. Windham and Dr. E. L. Strandell, who was the victim's attending physician." During that conversation, Taylor wrote, "The victim stated that one time the assault took place Sunday morning at the camp. When the victim was asked who made the assault, she stated that she did not remember. The victim stated that she did not remember anything that took place from early Saturday morning until her sister arrived at the camp to pick her up," on Sunday morning.

A week later, September 30th, sister Willie Mae Dawkins was interviewed at the DA's office. In the interview she stated "that at the time she and Lucille Jernigan drove up at the cabin on Sunday that Dr. Perry and Willie Stanley were already there and were in the process of unlocking the door." And that "Perry had a bottle of whiskey in one hand." The door, though, was latched from the inside. Willie Mae said, "Dr. Perry was telling Jean to get up and open the door," but she said, "I can't because I think my legs and left arm is paralyzed." Perry answered, "There's nothing wrong with you, get up and unlock the door." When Willie Mae saw "Jean lying in the kitchen floor I knew something was wrong." She asked Dr. Perry "if he couldn't take out a pane in the door, he said yes, but never made any effort to do so." She "then went to the door and took out one of the panes or rather I pushed one of them up so I could reach in and remove the night latch. I don't remember which pane it was but I do remember it was very easy to remove."

Inside, when asked what happened, Jean said, "I fell." Willie Mae "asked Dr. Perry if he couldn't do something for her, couldn't he see she was hurt. He said there was nothing wrong with her." Then she went into a back bedroom to get her sister's things, clothes, purse, describing the condition of the camp house, "the phone was off the table," a "bedspread or sheet in the living room," a "pillow and quilt" on one couch, "that looked like someone had slept there." In the bedroom "a lamp was knocked over and Jean's purse was open under the bed. Her cigarettes were in the floor and had been mashed. ... Her shoes were strewn across the floor, so was the white uniform she had worn away from home."

She said she "was in a hurry to get [Jean] away from there," and so didn't remember everything, but did "remember that Dr. Perry did not offer any assistance at all nor did he offer any help to see what was wrong with her." She and Willie got Jean's dress uniform back on her, which "usually fit loose but at the time they put it on Jean her stomach was swollen so much that they could not button" it. Once Jean was standing, she asked for a drink of water, but "strangled on it and it came back through her nose." With Willie's help they carried Jean to Lucille's car. She "could not use her feet at all hardly."

"On the way home," Willie Mae said, "I kept trying to get her to tell me what happened to her. She kept saying that she fell and I had to keep trying to get her to talk to keep her awake."

Lucille, interviewed on October 10th at the Colonial, painted essentially the same picture, saying they arrived at the cabin "approximately 9:50 A. M." found Perry and Willie already there, adding, "There was another bedspread on the floor in the bathroom," and "the trash can was turned over and trash was on the floor." Plus, she said, "After Willie Mae went to get Jeans' clothes, I asked Jean who did this to you and she said Dr. Perry."

Perry, interviewed on the 5th, "stated that when they got into the cabin he again told Jean to get up and she would not. He says that Lucille Jernigan and Willie picked Jean up and that nothing appears to be wrong with Jean except she is drunk." He "told them to put Jean on the bed and leave her there."

"Nice guy," Suzanne said.

"Has anyone else said anything about Jean drinking?" I asked.

"No. Perry's the only one with any alcohol so far—at nine-thirty on a Sunday morning."

"Wonder if they tested her for that at the hospital?"

"Would have been hours later."

"True."

Willie was interviewed the same day as Dr. Perry, and said he "was at the cabin with Dr. Perry when the victim was found on the kitchen floor," but "did not describe any injuries to the victim."

"Is that what he meant by 'I sure needed Willie's help'?"

"I thought he said, 'that night.'"

"Which night?"

"Let's keep reading."

Taylor recorded his conversation with Dr. Strandell in the hospital on his first visit, September 23rd. It was Buddy Windham, after seeing Jean's condition at their mother's house, who had called Strandell. Taylor wrote, "Dr. Strandell told me that Jean appeared to have been sexually assaulted," emphasizing, "my God ... I don't know where they sold tickets to this girl." In describing the injuries to her hip bones, Strandell "indicated and demonstrated 'it just looked like someone had used a hammer and pecked on both hip bones.'" Taylor then repeated the story of Strandell's withholding medication "until she told him what happened. She then told him that George Perry had beat her up."

On October 2nd, Jessie Ruth Holland, a nurse in the emergency room that day, was asked about the exchange, but could not corroborate it, saying she "did not hear Jean Barnes make any definite statements."

Buddy Windham remembered the scene this way in an October 6 interview: "Dr. Strandell inquired about what happened and said he would not touch her until the law was notified. Two city policemen were in the hospital," and they "called the Sheriff's Department. James Holmes and James Taylor," deputies, came to the hospital. "Dr. Strandell asked them where Scotty, Sheriff Byrne was. They said they didn't know. Dr. Strandell said you had better get him because George Perry has beat hell out of that Barnes girl and things are gong to get hotter than a potato." The deputies went into Jean's room for a few minutes. When they came back out, Buddy repeated "they had better get Scotty up there," but "they didn't say anything, just left." And that was the last time he saw "any law enforcement officials at the hospital until Friday," when Taylor showed up.

Monday, Lucille visited the hospital and Buddy told her he "couldn't find Sheriff Byrne." She called him and Buddy "talked to him by telephone. I asked him if he knew what was going on. He said that he had heard sketches of it," but wouldn't come to the hospital, and asked Buddy to come to his office "at dinner time," instead. "[T]here would be nobody there but him and [they] could talk about it."

At his office, "he wanted to know what had happened," and Buddy "told him that she had been beaten up. He asked if she said George Perry did it. I told him yes. He said he had talked with George Perry and George had told him that he had been in Pensacola on Saturday night."

"Here we go," I said.

"What else?"

"Scotty said if Jean would sign a warrant for George Perry that he would arrest him."

"And?"

"And, nothing." When asked if he "could get someone in here on it," Scotty gave him an "FBI number."

When he called the number, an agent "said that State Investigator Taylor was suppose to have done been in there."

But it wasn't until a phone call that Friday, from a friend of Buddy's, Lloyd Hart, that brought Taylor to Brewton. "This is interesting," I said, flipping to Pete's account.

At approximately 12:00 noon Friday September 23, 1966 Corporal R. C. Taylor was in Monroeville, Alabama and received a telephone call from Lloyd Hart in Brewton. Mr. Hart told Corporal Taylor there was a woman in the hospital in Brewton that had been beaten and was addicted to narcotics. Mr. Hart stated that this woman was willing to sign a deposition, warrant or affidavit or whatever might be required. He asked Corporal Taylor to come to Brewton and investigate the matter. I told Mr. Hart I would leave Monroeville shortly and would contact him when I arrived in Brewton. A few minutes after this telephone conversation with Mr. Hart I was notified by radio that Sheriff Byrne of Brewton wished to see me. I had him advised that I was enroute to Brewton from Monroeville and would contact him when I got there. Upon arriving in Brewton at approximately 1:30 P. M. I went to the Sheriff's Office. The Sheriff had left town, he was contacted by radio and requested to call his office by telephone. I talked to the Sheriff by telephone and he asked me to make an investigation into the matter concerning Jean Barnes.

"Interesting isn't the word for it," Suzanne said.

"Now, now."

"Anything else about a warrant?"

"No," I said, "despite Jean's repeatedly claiming Perry beat her up."

Ralph Windham, Jean's brother, asked her "who in the world did all this to you." She replied, "Perry beat me up." Delores Bagwell asked Jean, "who did this," that Friday in the hospital. At the mention of Perry's name, "tears came into Jean's eyes." Then, according to Bagwell, "Jean said Delores you are just like me, you wouldn't believe it either if I told you."

On Tuesday afternoon, Francis Burch, a private duty nurse, "asked her 'who in the name of Heaven did this?'" Jean answered, "It was George."

"What did Perry say to that?" Suzanne asked.

I found the pages of Perry's interview. "After being advised of his rights Dr. Perry told investigators that he had practiced medicine in Brewton for several years. He attended medical schools at the University of Alabama and Louisville, Kentucky, from 1935 to 1941. He has served as coroner for Escambia County since 1948 or 1949," about the time he married Marguerite and George Jr. was born.

"Dr. Perry advised that he had been going with the victim Jean Barnes for approximately five years," since about 1961. "Mrs. Perry has known for about three years that he was dating the victim." They'd had divorce papers filled out twice, but didn't go through with it because Marguerite "wanted all the property including the office building." But they had an agreement: "[H]e would stay home on Monday and Friday nights. Most of the other nights were spent at the cabin with the victim."

"Good old Brewton," Suzanne sighed.

"On Friday September 16, 1966 Dr. Perry states that he made a telephone call at approximately 11:30 P. M. This call was made to Jean Barnes at the White Horse Inn. Jean was working this night." He said he "made arrangements with Jean to meet her at her house at 11:45." He went to her house, but she didn't show up. He went to his office, called Jean, they talked, then "she came to Dr. Perry's office, arriving there sometime after 1:00 A. M. He said she "fell up the steps," that "she was drunk when she arrived at his office. He called Willie to come to the office. They "put Jean in Dr. Perry's car," and "drove directly to Jean's home on Gillis Street."

They argued, "had a scuffle trying to get Jean into the house." Jean's mother stated that she saw Perry slap her daughter during the scuffle. Unrepentant, Perry told Willie "that if he was going to have to stay here all night he wanted a drink," and sent him back to the office for a bottle of whiskey." While Willie was gone, Perry, Jean's mother, and then Jean went into the house.

He and Mrs. Windham "sat down on the couch and Jean went into her bedroom. Shortly she came out carrying two pieces of clothing in her hand." Perry said Jean "had called a cab" and gone outside to meet it. He went back to his office shortly after, "got into his son's car and drove home."

He was back at the office by 9:30 the next morning, "remaining there until 12:30" when he went home to lunch, staying there until 2. At 4:30 he and Mack Nelson left for Florida, to the Rainbow Café, in Pensacola, run by Laura Hill, a woman Perry "had gone with" fifteen years earlier, and another woman named Hazel. After the club closed, they all went to Laura's house. Perry said he was drunk, and so "did not know what time they left" Pensacola, but "arrived back in Brewton at 8:10 Sunday morning," Nelson driving him to Willie's house. Perry said he was asleep when they got to Willie's, but that "Willie later told him it was 8:10 A. M. when they arrived." Willie drove him to his office while Perry slept some more in the car. "When he woke up he and Willie [went] out to the cabin."

Suzanne stopped me. "Went to the cabin? Why?"

"Doesn't say."

"He's so drunk he's passing out in the car, and he wants to go to his cabin?"

Perry reiterated much of the scene at the camp, Willie Mae and Lucille arriving "immediately" after he did, the night latch, Willie Mae taking "out one of the glass slats," to get inside. After they'd gotten Jean dressed and into Lucille's car, Perry "called his wife by telephone at her house and told her to come to the camp." Marguerite said in her interview that she did not see Perry from when he left the office Saturday afternoon until "he called her on the telephone about 9:30 A. M. Sunday and told her there was trouble at the camp."

She stopped me again. "Nine-thirty?"

"What it says."

Mack Nelson said they left Laura Hill's house "sometime after daylight," Mack driving, and Perry asleep. "He drove straight to Willie Stanley's house in Brewton." At Willie's house, Mack "got the keys to his station wagon," which was parked there. He "went straight home, getting there just before 10:00 A. M. Nelson was asked if he was sure of the time of his arrival at home to which he replied, 'Yes, I am sure it was just before 10:00 A. M.' He stated that his wife reamed his ass out because she wanted him to go to church and it was too late," the service starting at ten.

Laura Hill, Hazel, and Bill Crawford, who "plays the guitar and sings with the band" at the café were interviewed together. They said Nelson and Perry got to the café about 8, Saturday night, where they "ate fish for supper, drank some and danced." It was "approximately 2:30 or 2:45" when they closed up the café and went to Laura's house. She and Hazel said "it was sometime after daylight" when Nelson and Perry left, later stating "it was from 7:00 to 9:00 A. M. Sunday morning."

With just a little calculating, I said, "Not exactly what you'd call air tight."

"What I want to know is," she answered, "does anyone else offer an explanation of what did happen at the camp, if Perry wasn't there and didn't beat her up?"

"Let me see," I said. "Just this, from Gardner's notes: He says Lucille 'took Dr. Perry aside and asked him if he did it,' that Sunday at the cabin. 'He was either drunk or doped up at the time and he tried to get nasty with her, and said no, he had been in Pensacola.' And then, 'Lucille's theory is that Jean had tried to play on people's sympathy before, and that she was so doped up or drunk that she kept falling and probably burned herself trying to light cigarettes.' And then, I don't know why, he writes, 'Lucille says it was around 4 A. M. when Jean Barnes called a taxi and got her car from near Dr. P's office, later driving to cabin.' Lucille wasn't there when she called the cab, was she?"

"Not that anyone's mentioned."

"Why in the hell would he note that?" I said, going back to Lucille's statement. "She doesn't say anything about Friday night."

"Or they didn't ask her."

"Possibly, but she volunteered plenty of other stuff. Listen to this: 'One time at the cabin, she,' Jean, 'knocked him down and then kicked him on the seat.'"

"Good for her," Suzanne said.

"It gets better: 'Dr. Perry went and got his gun and pointed it at Jean. I believe he told her he would kill her.' And this: 'Dr. Perry has called Lucille by telephone. One time since she saw him at the cabin the Sunday morning that Jean was found, he told her in the telephone conversation not to lie for him, that he had done nothing to hide'."

"Wouldn't you love to have heard that conversation?" I said.

"Wonder if she testified to the Grand Jury."

"Sounds like it wouldn't have mattered. If all the evidence that is in there wasn't enough to raise suspicions, what would?"

"True," Suzanne said. "Anybody say anything about the day she died?"

"Other than the newspaper account?"

"Yeah. Anything about either of the stories Willie Mae told?"

From the nieces we were told about a phantom phone call. But then Willie Mae said Annie Jean was alone that morning.

"Hmm," I said, scanning the report. "Just this, again, from the October 31st interview Taylor had with Strandell: who 'stated that in talking to the victim's mother, Mrs. Lovie Windham that she said that she had just left Jean's bedside to go to the bathroom. Jean was apparently alright when she left. Dr. Strandell says that Mrs. Windham stated that she would not have been gone more than three minutes. She came back and noticed that Jean was having trouble with her breathing. She immediately called the nurses and they came and the nurses then called Dr. Strandell.' He was in his office, just behind the hospital, but by the time he arrived, she was dead, and attempts to revive her failed."

Suzanne shook her head, exasperated. "Everybody's got a different story."

"Looks like."

"Anything else?"

"Copies of the newspaper articles; nothing much new. And it looks like part of Perry's phone records."

"What's that about?"

"Says Perry 'has made several telephone calls to Pensacola since he came back from' there. He called the Rainbow club from his cabin on September 14th, the 20th, and the 21st. Told Taylor he was trying to organize a band."

"A band?"

"Yeah, said he was calling Pensacola to 'arrange for the two women and the singer,'—I guess that would be Laura, Hazel and Crawford—'to play at the White Horse Inn.' Said 'Carolyn Hazelett wanted the band to play at the White Horse Inn four nights a week'." I looked up from the report. "Who's Carolyn Hazelett?"

"Ran the place."

Then I noticed something else. "This is strange. If they pulled phone records from the cabin, and show calls on the 14th and the 20th, where's Annie Jean's call on the 18th?"

"No shit."

"And listen to this: 'On Saturday night September 24, 1966 Carolyn Hazelett was interviewed at the White Horse Inn.'"

"The same day Jean died? That's curious. What'd she say?"

"During this interview Carolyn stated that at 11:30 P. M. Friday night September 16, 1966, that Doc Perry called to the White Horse Inn by telephone. He wanted to speak to Jean Barnes and Jean talked to him on the phone. Jean got off from work at the White Horse at 1:00 A. M."

"Wait a minute," Suzanne said. "Didn't Perry say he made arrangements to meet Jean at 11:45?"

"Says here the time was confirmed by two cooks at the White Horse. Jean was scheduled to work that Saturday night, 'but did not show up.' At 1:10 in the afternoon on Sunday, Perry called the White Horse from his cabin. 'Carolyn said that Doc sounded very drunk. Had some sarcastic remarks to make so Carolyn said that she would not talk to him.' About 4 P. M. on Monday, 'Perry came into the White Horse Inn and used the telephone. He called the Rainbow Inn in Pensacola,' charging the call 'to his number at the cabin.' He asked to speak to Crawford, was given another number, got no answer there, and called the Rainbow back."

"This about the so-called band?"

"Doesn't say anything about a band yet."

"'Arrangements were made for Perry's chauffer who is Willie Stanley to go to Pensacola the following afternoon and meet these two women and Bill Crawford at the bus station.' Willie went, waited there for two hours, but they never showed up. 'Carolyn stated that at the time Perry made this phone call to Pensacola to arrange for the two women and Bill Crawford to come up, either just before making this phone call or just after he made it Doc Perry told Carolyn that he had an alibi where he was Saturday night. He said he could prove where he was. Carolyn stated that Doc was in the White Horse Inn Monday and Tuesday afternoon September 19, 20 1966. She says this is the first time that Doc Perry has been into the White Horse Inn in over a year'."

"Wait a minute," Suzanne said again. "He's telling Carolyn on Monday the 19th that he has an alibi, when no one started investigating until the 23rd?"

"Yup."

"So he was trying to bring those folks up from Pensacola to verify his alibi two and a half weeks before he was interviewed."

"Here we go: They came into the White Horse on the 21st, 'two big women from Pensacola and a boy named Bill Crawford.' Carolyn says they sat at a table and 'Dr. Perry joined them.' He told her he wanted to meet, quote, 'about forming a band to play at the White Horse Inn, at Jack Martin's place and other places.' But then Carolyn told Taylor 'that she had not at any time talked to Dr. Perry in reference to the forming of a band to play at her place. She stated that she did not want a band there and had made no arrangements to get one. She also owns Jack Martin's place,' which already had a band, and she wasn't 'interested in getting a new one.'"

"His story's full of holes."

"Jesus," I said.

"What?"

"Carolyn stated that on September 26, 1966 George Perry called Beco, where Jean worked to see if they had any insurance on Jean."

"Asking for the family, the kids?"

"Maybe. But both Willie Mae and Jean's mother said they told him they didn't want to talk to him in the days after she died. This is the same Monday afternoon he's calling the Rainbow."

"Taylor wrote that?"

"Notes of the interview."

"Thought they didn't ask about insurance?"

"That's what he told us," I said. "And that's not the first time it came up. Willie Mae wrote in her statement that Jean told her several times that if Perry died, she'd get the camp house, and was the beneficiary of a $10,000 policy he had."

"What the hell?"

"Sounds a little like that story he told us, remember—two ABI agents having an affair, taking out policies for each other."

"Anything else?"

"No. That's pretty much it. Lots of short statements from people about the drug racket in Brewton."

"Drug racket, for a homicide investigation?"

"I know," I said, scanning. Albert Jackson and Francis Burch's cousin, Robert Bagwell, came forward and said they had information about the Barnes case. Then they just repeat what Francis told them. "Get this: 'During the interview,' on October 9th, `Mr. Jackson and Mr. Baggett were asked if they knew of any place in or around Brewton selling narcotics or pills. They both gave a negative answer to the question'."

"What does that have to do with Annie Jean?"

I kept reading. "On October 8th, Ed McCall was interviewed, and it was his belief that narcotics were being sold at 'Mutt Rawls's Place.' Lucille Jernigan's name comes up, as providing pills. Daryl Weeks was interviewed. Mrs. Coy Lee Newsom, 'believes that the sheriff Scotty Byrne is taking dope. He came to her house one time to pick up some property that her husband had taken from the paper mill.' And, 'Some time before Jean Barnes died, she told Mrs. Newsom that Coy Lee Newsom was involved in a dope ring with Johney Faye Humphrey.' Mrs. Newsom named Lucille in that same ring. But then, they interviewed Glen Holt on the 13th, and he said, 'I have more trouble out of the Newsoms and the Weeks than all of the other town put together. They are always calling and complaining.' Although, Gardner talked to a Dr. Low, who 'feels she is telling the truth, and her story should be checked out'."

"I don't get it."

"Here we go. From Gardner's notes of a discussion with Mrs. Newsom: 'In the weeks just prior to the Barnes incident, she had Jean Barnes checking on her husband for her, I guess. After several visits back to her beauty shop, Jean Barnes told her she could no longer be seen with her. ... that she (Jean) was afraid, and that Dot's life was in danger. A few days after their last contact, Jean is admitted to the hospital.'"

"Why was Jean checking on Coy Lee?" Suzanne asked. "Could she have been beaten up for drug stuff?"

"She was afraid of someone."

"Wonder who they nabbed in the drug indictments? If there's a connection, wouldn't that be enough for the D.A. to give up the Grand Jury testimony?"

"I think there're enough questions and curiosities in here," I said, waving the report, "we can push like hell."

"I'm with you," Suzanne said. Then, "Wait," as I was sliding the bundle back into its envelope. "Just for kicks, is there any mention of Dickson or Hanson in there?"

"Dickson or Hanson?"

"You know, the other agents Chief Jones sent down, supposedly, because of Taylor's familiarity with Scotty."

"Oh, right," I said, sifting through the pages again. The only other agents mentioned were E. J. Dixon and Herman Chapman. "Surely, that's who he meant, don't you think?"

"Sure, probably. Except they both lived in Brewton then, still do. No reason to think they weren't just as familiar with Scotty, if that was such an issue."

"Still live in Brewton, as in still alive?"

"Far as I know."

Murder Creek

Probable Cause

PROBABLE CAUSE IS the benchmark for a grand jury's return of an indictment, or a "true bill," as it's formally called. The grand jury is one of the oldest constitutionally recognized legal institutions. It was included in the Magna Carta, the first English constitutional document, granted in 1215. "The first English grand jury consisted of twelve men selected from the knights or other freemen who were summoned to inquire into crimes alleged to have been committed in their local community. Thus, grand jurors originally functioned as accusers or witnesses, rather than as judges."

Critical elements of the modern grand jury, as it's practiced here, developed much earlier in England. Its proceedings became secret, one of its most important aspects, after a long hard fight, achieving an independence from the Crown. "As a result, a grand jury is able to vote an indictment or refuse to do so, as it deems proper, without regard to the recommendations of judge, prosecutor, or any other person."

English colonists brought the institution to America. The "tradition of the grand jury was well established in the American colonies long before the American Revolution. Indeed, the colonists used it as a platform from which to assert their independence from the pressures of colonial governors. In 1735, for example, the Colonial Governor of New York demanded that a grand jury indict for libel John Zenger, editor of a newspaper called The Weekly Journal, because he had held up to scorn certain acts of the Royal Governor. The grand jury flatly refused."

The grand jury was so well established it was included in the Bill of Rights. "The Fifth Amendment to the Constitution of the United States provides in part that '[n]o person shall be held to answer for a capital, or otherwise infamous crime, unless on a presentment or indictment of a Grand Jury.'"[37]

Murder Creek

A grand jury doesn't determine guilt or innocence. Rather, it determines, only, whether there is probable cause to believe that a crime was committed and that a specific person committed it. I read between those co-joined requirements—a crime being committed and a specific person committing it—the loophole through which Annie Jean's case disappeared. If there was no crime, there can be no criminal. Having determined that Jean's death resulted from natural causes, that is, they found no demonstrable indication that criminal behavior resulted in her death. A "homicide" investigation was consequently emptied of any purpose, became little more than a formality. Once they have Perry's alibi, that's it. Other than Marguerite Perry, who tells them she doesn't know of anyone else was out there that Saturday, not a single other person rumored to have been at the camp that weekend was interviewed—despite not giving up any names, Suzanne could confirm none of them showed up in the report—though investigators followed up on all those rumors pertaining to Brewton's alleged drug racket. Why is that, and how is it possible?

After reading the investigative report, I understood better the comments included in the published grand jury report, especially the line, "We believe that every citizen is entitled to a prompt, courteous, and efficient investigation of their complaint," a line that echoes the ABI's motto of "Courtesy, Service, Protection," too closely to ignore. There's not much evidence to suggest Annie Jean's case was investigated promptly. And there's enough doubt as to its efficiency to ask, How well was that citizen protected?

But the real question at that point became, once the evidence was turned over to the grand jury, what were their options? Page two of The United States Courts' Handbook says the "grand jury's work is concerned with evidence brought to its attention by an attorney for the government." While they "may consider additional matters," they "should consult" with the prosecuting attorney or the court "before undertaking a formal investigation" on its own (emphasis added).

Twenty-three people were selected for the grand jury. In the proceedings of November 14, 1966, members were culled from a list of 70 potential candidates. Sixteen jurors constitute a quorum, and must be present during any business transacted. It takes twelve affirmative votes to hand down an indictment. Once the jury is sworn and charged, witnesses are called to testify. No one else is allowed in the courtroom, other than the jurors, judge, state attorney, recorder, and witness. Witnesses may be excused during questioning to seek clarification or counsel from a defense attorney, but that attorney is not permitted inside.

"It is the responsibility of the grand jury to weigh the evidence presented to it in order to determine whether this evidence, usually without any explanation being offered by the accused"— in fact, the accused does not have to testify, and is usually dissuaded from doing so—"persuades it that there is probable cause to believe that a crime has been committed and that the accused was the person who committed it. Remember that the grand jury is not responsible for determining whether the accused is guilty beyond a reasonable doubt, but only whether there is sufficient evidence of probable cause to justify bringing the accused to trial."[38] Hence, Wachtler's "ham sandwich" remark.

The other side of that, though, holds that "no one can be prosecuted for a serious crime unless the grand jury decides that the evidence it has heard so requires. In this way, the grand jury operates both as a 'sword,' authorizing the government's prosecution of suspected criminals, and also as a 'shield,' protecting citizens from unwarranted or inappropriate prosecutions"[39]: the Rule of Law.

That law "imposes upon each grand juror a strict obligation of secrecy. This obligation is emphasized in the oath each grand juror takes and in the charge given to the grand jury by the judge," and the scope of that secrecy is unambiguous: "Essentially, the grand jury may disclose matters occurring before it only to the attorneys for the government for use in the performance of their duties, but even attorneys for the government may not be informed of what took place during the grand jury's deliberations and voting. The only other time matters occurring before the grand jury may be disclosed to anyone is when disclosure is ordered by the court in the interests of justice."[40]

"Doesn't look good," I said to Suzanne.

"Can we make any claim to the 'interests of justice'?"

"I doubt it, if only because of practical limitations, at this point. I mean, we could argue that Annie Jean was denied justice, and by extension her family was. But I'll bet any DA will fall back on procedure. There's no way."

"All we can do is ask."

"See if anything shakes out."

The rule of law, it's said, has at least three meanings. First, it is a regulator of governmental power. Second, it means equality before the law. And last, the rule of law means procedural and formal justice. Annie Jean had been denied justice on at least two of those counts, and the third looked to prevent us from rectifying that.

And then I saw this quote in the newspaper: Baldwin County attorney Wilson Myers was returning to Iraq, where he'd spent a year previously helping the country build a "stable and fair" legal system. "A country's rule of law system is from bottom to top," Myers was quoted. "You have to have citizens who believe in the judicial system and believe in the police as being honest members of society."[41] What would he say, I wondered, about the proceedings in Brewton, little more than an hour away, versus thousands of miles? I know the lesson those citizens on the bottom took from the apparent mishandling—something the grand jury itself did allude to, but were quick to add that no "pay-off" or "cover-up" occurred, a curious protestation whose origins, whatever they were, engender not confidence, but pause—of Annie Jean's case. But would that be enough of an appeal to prompt a DA to reexamine the case though?

Kenneth Taylor had told me that only a DA or circuit judge could authorize release of the grand jury's proceedings. The current Escambia County DA, we found out, was Steve Billy. And the current circuit judge was Bradley Byrne, Scotty's son.

"Should we go to Bradley?" I asked. "See if that gets a response from Scotty?"

"I don't think I'm ready for that."

We called Billy's office, set up an appointment. My feeling was that if Billy denied our request, the only other opportunity to get at the truth would be through Scotty, but we hadn't been able to get to him yet. If, say, word got out that we'd been through the forensics reports, and the ABI report, were asking questions about the grand jury, would he want to go on record with an explanation or clarification of his own?

That was a central purpose to pursuing the story, I felt. There were enough holes in the official version, enough inexplicable gaps, that a person who could fill them in, and had been carrying that information around for forty years, would want to, wouldn't they? And wouldn't that, in turn, free George Jr. to leave Brewton for good, a place he is so otherwise completely at odds with? Wouldn't that permit Joyce and Ralph, the rest of Annie Jean's children, to look forward, finally?

We met Billy on a Thursday afternoon, early August, the season's first tropical storm to take aim on the Gulf threatening to intensify to hurricane strength the same day. On the way to Brewton we rehearsed possible exchanges with the DA, assuming the worst, assuming officious reluctance, or preoccupied indifference, just to be safe, safe from the possibility of allowing unprotected naiveté to spoil what little chance we thought we had.

"What do we want?" I asked, taking on the role of Billy.

"The grand jury proceedings, testimony, report."

"Why?"

"For her children's sake, because they never knew what happened."

"Do we tell him about the book?"

"Sure."

I was wary of prejudicing him in any way, worried that the prospect of an actual publication documenting our efforts would cause him to be more guarded than he might otherwise be, or worse, that he'd view us as capitalizing on the story, and any reluctance on his part would morph into hostility.

Book editors and agents, often, because of the sheer volume of submissions they receive, are looking for any reason not to contract or represent a project. An operating principle in the process of writing, then, becomes not giving them that reason. "Make it bullet proof," a writer friend has characterized the approach. There was no reason not to take the same stance with Billy. "Gives us some moral high ground, even," Suzanne assured me, "with the children getting a cut of the proceeds."

"Okay. That's good. But what makes us think the records should be looked at again?"

"Justice," she said.

"That's going to be a sticking point," I thought. "What if he says no?"

"Then we go to a judge."

"Byrne?"

"Does it have to be the circuit judge?" Suzanne had a friend, the same friend, in fact, who shared the story about the DJ going silent, that'd spawned Temple, who was a district judge in another part of the state.

"I don't know. We should try to find out the pecking order, the procedure, without letting on why we want to know."

Such paranoia came from being too close to the story, I tried to tell myself, after we'd stopped for lunch and was in the restroom to wash up. "You're going crazy," I said to my mirrored likeness. Then I thought, hell, he could cancel on us, not bother with it at all.

But he didn't. The door to his office was closed, dark, and locked up when we got there, fifteen minutes early. A guard said they were still at lunch. We could wait in the hallway, on the chairs outside the courtroom. A couple of minutes later he came down the opposite hallway, paused at his office door, and then walked by us.

"That him?" I asked, after he'd disappeared into an ante room.

"I don't know."

The guard told the man we were waiting for him.

"Must be," I answered myself, rising from the chair.

He came back out, extended a hand and started to say, "Steve Billy," when recognition changed his demeanor. "Oh, hey, Suzanne!"

He'd been a childhood friend with one of her younger brothers.

They shared a hug and he welcomed us into the office suite, through another door, "Have a seat," apologizing for the clutter before closing the door. They caught up on some of the years that had passed, how he had gone from florist to lawyer, their respective parents, siblings, and children, Suzanne's writing, before she said, "Joe's writing most of this book."

He said he wasn't very familiar with the case, which was a little disappointing, though maybe only because I'd primed myself for both resistance, and, to be honest, something like enthusiasm. His secretary had said, "Tell me what you want to meet about," when we'd made the appointment, "in case I need to pull any files for him." And, he added, he didn't really remember knowing anything about it at the time.

"You were probably too young," Suzanne said.

"Yeah, probably out committing my own crimes," he said, and laughed.

He was an affable, relaxed guy, with a quick, crooked grin, shirt sleeves, loose tie, hair styled on the longish and casual side of things. He wasn't much on formality, and not unreceptive, listening to the story, asking probing questions but not challenging any interpretation we offered.

After I detailed Jean's injuries, both Shoffeitt's and Strandell's arguably inconsistent accounts, he asked, "But there was no indictment?" the first sign of surprise in his voice.

"No. What's more, there was no one charged," I said.

"Not even Perry, after she'd named him?"

"He had an alibi," I told him, explaining it, and its apparent gaps. "That's one of the things we wanted to talk with you about. How does that work, exactly? What were the jury's options in a case like that?"

"Well," he started, "the only thing a grand jury can do is examine the evidence put before them," straight out of the handbook.

"But that's the problem," I said. "If the investigators are calling it a homicide case, then forensics says she died of natural causes, and no one is charged, would it even have been possible to hand down an indictment?"

"No," he said, then thought a moment. "Probably not."

"That's why we'd sure like to get a look at what evidence was presented."

"This is what year?"

"Sixty-six."

"Who was DA then, Wiley?"

"Right. Henderson." That prompted another of those grins. "He played the game a little bit differently," he said, shaking his head. "He used to keep all his files at home. When he retired, he wanted the next DA—Mike," he said, gesturing to Suzanne, "to come out to his house and copy them. What a nightmare. I don't know if he did that, shredded them, or what."

"His case files?" I asked, for clarification. "Not the jury transcripts."

"Right."

"Beause I talked with Kenneth Taylor, and he sounded pretty sure they were in storage."

"Could be. Could be. Was there a published report?" he asked.

"Yeah. They said at the time, that after examining all the evidence they found no reason to take any action," I told him, paraphrasing. "Though they did scold the sheriff's department a little, saying every citizen deserved, how did they put it, 'prompt, courteous and efficient investigation of their complaint'."

"Where'd that come from?"

"Exactly." I told him about the five days the family tried to get someone to talk to Jean, to take her statement, about her brother having to track down the sheriff.

"Which brother?" he asked. "Buddy?"

"Right."

"He's a good guy. Used to come in the flower shop all the time," he said to Suzanne.

I told him it was only after Buddy's friend, Lloyd Hart's phone call—because Hart had experience with the narcotics folks at I&I—that anyone started investigating the case. And then something stuck out about that whole sequence of events, which I hadn't paid enough attention to before, but I didn't mention it yet.

"Wow," he said. "Sure sounds like they dropped the ball, didn't follow through, because they considered her, thought she was,"

"Disposable," I volunteered.

"Right."

"From the wrong side of the creek, just East Brewton white trash," Suzanne offered. They shared a knowing glance.

"And yet, the last line of the report says, 'We also want to exonerate the sheriff personally, from any implication in any case brought before us.'"

"What in the world?"

"And this: 'it is the opinion and findings of state investigators and this grand jury,' that they found no evidence of any 'pay-off' of Escambia County officials, nor any indication of a 'cover-up' of any evidence."

"Where'd that come from?" he repeated, straightening up in his chair a bit, genuine befuddlement clouding his face.

"Yeah. We thought that quite odd."

"Now I'm curious to see what's in the file."

"What's the procedure for that?" Suzanne asked. "Do we need to go to a judge?"

"That's a bit tricky in this case," he said, rubbing his head. "The judge now is the son of the sheriff then, Scotty Byrne."

I almost laughed at myself. I'd gone out of my way to not mention Scotty's name: more of that paranoia. Steve caught my grin, but didn't ask about it.

"I'll talk to Mike, see what he says."

"Remind him," Suzanne said, "that we used to talk about the case before he was a lawyer, used to say we'd solve it some day."

"Really?" he asked, then shifted into more of a DA mode. "Probably couldn't have brought a murder charge, because she was admitted to the hospital, had been getting treatment, improving," he said. "Manslaughter, maybe. Or aggravated assault."

"Seems like they could have charged assault, at the very least," I said.

"True," he said, puzzling over the issue. "Tell you what, I'll look into it, see what's there."

"Do you think we'll be able to look at it, too?" I asked.

"As far as I'm concerned, yeah, I don't see why not, what with it being so long ago, with the victim, the possible accused being dead. Is there anyone still alive that could be accused?"

"Well, yeah, there's a handful of guys still around, if what we think might've happened is true," I told him, without mentioning any names. We had a theory about part of an explanation for Jean's injuries, but were waiting on an expert's opinion.

"Some folks, like Bradley—I know Brad—he's likely to say the chips fell where they fell, why not leave it at that, if there's no chance to correct it."

We'd certainly heard similar sentiment, both directly, and second-hand, from Lonnie Barnes to Hugh Caffey. I'd even been told, more generally, that it's a peculiarly Southern attitude—that "the past is past," and not worth worrying over too much. "Right," I had answered. "The same South where Civil War re-enactments are still staged?"

But the point can easily be made that there are more important, immediate, even life-and-death concerns to be addressed: the possibility of another hurricane striking the Gulf Coast, a prime example. But something about the story, about Brewton, where the dividing lines separating race and class distinctions are still so physically obvious and temperamentally adhered to, where you're almost always within walking distance of both blatant privilege and suffering deprivation, I wondered how much of it could possibly be excused as mere preference—remembering Mary Tucker's comments—versus the same old entrenched, Alabama hierarchy, enabled by, and protected within, the 1901 Constitution. Michael Harrington, in The Other America, had some pretty damning things to say about such elitist attitudes:

The individual cannot usually break out of this vicious circle [of poverty]. Neither can the group, for it lacks the social energy and political strength to turn its misery into a cause. Only the larger society, with its help and resources, can really make it possible for these people to help themselves. Yet those who could make the difference too often refuse to act because of their ignorant, smug moralisms. They view the effects of poverty—above all, the warping of the will and spirit that is a consequence of being poor—as choices. (p. 15)

The larger society, in this case the State of Alabama, had no intention of sharing, or offering resources, or help. The constitution insured that governmental power, the control of resources—even how they could be utilized on the local level—was seated in the center of that government, with the legislature, in Montgomery, in the hands of "the intelligent and virtuous."

But Harrington was writing in the early sixties, and ordinarily you'd expect things to change, improve. Writing as late as the fall of 2005, James Wolcott had this to say:

The true eye-opener from Katrina was having the flap lifted on the specter of lower-depths poverty in this country. All those poor people—where'd they come from? They've been kept under wraps for so long that seeing them massed or queued for food stamps and A.T.M. cards was like having a family secret escape from the cellar.

In fact, he goes on to suggest that things have gotten worse, if anything:

Poverty has been scrubbed from the American screen with a sanitary wipe. The New York Times can publish chastening headlines about the poverty rate rising under President Bush, but those numbers remain abstractions until faces and bodies apply flesh to them. Network news and reality shows oscillate between salivating over celebrity bling and fretting about the middle-class squeeze (climbing health-care costs, etc.) but those down in the basement of the American Dream might as well be mole people for all the attention they draw.

And Wolcott registers a bit of frustration, or incredulity, that it should be so, that Harrington's clarion call had been given no more credence than it has over the last two generations: "Summing up the majority attitude toward the poor in his famous review of Michael Harrington's The Other America, Dwight Macdonald said that 'poor people never seem able to obtain traction; things are always going wrong for them; their problems are so complicated—face it, they're a bringdown, man.' Which is why America ignores them as much as possible, until it's no longer possible and the conscience is nagged,"[42] until "the flap", the nefarious veil is lifted, as W.E.B. Du Bois famously said.

Because no matter how many laws and customs are struck down in an effort to level the playing field—as was earnestly attempted in the immediate wake of Harrington's book, suffrage rights were federally mandated, Alabama's poll tax was finally struck down, its schools finally integrated, its judiciary was transformed from a laughing-stock to respectability—if only one team has the keys to the gate and access to the equipment, they'll just keep rephrasing the rules to suit their purposes. So long as that's the case, the serious and immediate concerns of one— preparing one's mansions for a storm, say, to stick with the theme, where one might want to jet off to in the event of an evacuation, and securing one's insurance status—are not the same for the other. Sometimes it takes such a storm for that point to become evident. But it shouldn't.

Which is why I said to District Attorney Billy, "Yeah, we've been told as much. But Brad wouldn't think that if he talked to her kids."

Suzanne shot me a look.

"Why do you say that?" he answered.

"In a lot of ways, it might as well still be 1966 for them."

To which he nodded, said, "Yeah, I can understand that."

You can see it in their faces, hear it in their voices, how much they've been stunted by the story. The yearning in Ralph's, Joyce's, and Brenda's questions are dulled by age and as such marked by time, by the decades they've been asking those questions. Even Lonnie, who's petulant reluctance to revisit what he only knew as an awful fairy tale at the time, reduces him—grown, hulking in his middle age—to the baby of the family.

And George, his reaction and revulsion to the story carries with it the agitation of a teenager's sudden awakening to the injustices beyond his world, not the measured contemplation of someone who's been practicing law for thirty years. He might as well be still trying to reconcile the chasm separating a DC dining hall and the back door to a Montgomery barbecue joint.

Mr. Billy didn't say much else about the protocol for what we were asking, just that he'd look into it, get back to us. He did say it'd probably be best if Jean's children made the formal request. We exchanged contact information, thanked him, and left.

In the hallway, a cluster of men stood conferring at the top of the staircase. As we stepped past them, I overheard one of them address a tall, trim, dignified looking gentleman with gray, thinning hair, as Judge. I took another look at the man as we rounded the landing between floors, wondering if he was Bradley Byrne. In a perfect world, I thought, for the briefest of moments, I could approach the man, could say, "Judge, we're just looking for the truth..." and he would understand. Then I remembered where I was.

Once back in the car, cruising through Brewton, Suzanne asked me, "What was that about?"

"What?"

"That line about Jean's kids."

"About it still being sixty-six for them?"

"Yeah."

"I don't know. I guess I was just trying to provoke him a little."

"Why would you do that?"

"He didn't strike me as being real aggressive. When he didn't put up any fight, I was hoping to spark something like indignation, make him an advocate for the kids, you know."

"He's a good guy."

"Oh, he seemed like a very nice guy."

"Then just wait, give him a chance."

"You're right, you're right. I thought of something in there, though, made me anxious."

"What?"

"When I was telling him about the week she was in the hospital, Hart's phone call, Perry's alibi."

"He picked up on that, how he was offering an alibi before anyone asked."

"It's more than that."

"Explain."

"Look at all the pieces," I said, glad that she was driving, so I might be able to lay the whole puzzle out. "The same day that Perry's telling Carolyn Hazelett that he's got an alibi, Scotty tells Buddy he talked to George, and George told him he was in Pensacola."

"Yeah?"

"Well, first of all, if he's not investigating the case, what's Scotty doing talking to Perry about it? And what's the possibility they cooked up his story together?"

"Perry called Pensacola on the 14th, the Wednesday before she went out to the camp."

"Right, on or about the same day she's telling Dot Newsom she's afraid for her life."

"Did she say that?" Suzanne challenged me. "Did she say she was afraid for her life, or Dot's life?"

"Correct, I stand corrected. She only said she was afraid, that Dot's life was in danger."

"You got to be tight with this stuff."

"You're right," I said. "But then, there's no official investigation started until the next Friday, after Scotty gives Buddy the FBI number, the FBI tells him Taylor was supposed to be in Brewton—but on a narcotics investigation, right, and Taylor told us they were already on that—Buddy goes to Hart with Taylor's name, Hart calls Taylor, tells him there's a woman in the hospital, beaten and addicted, linking the two, and Taylor says he'll be there in an hour. As soon as he's on the road from Monroeville, he gets a call from the Brewton sheriff's department, that they want him to investigate the case. Do you think that's just a coincidence?"

"Yes, there is that chance."

"Damn, you're tough."

"I'm telling you, we have to be. Go on."

"Pete goes to Hart's store, then to the hospital with Buddy. He talks to Jean, Buddy, Jean's mother, and Strandell. He's a narcotics guy, but Buddy told the newspaper no one asked him about what he'd taken out of Jean's purse for another week, after she died."

"So?"

Murder Creek

"So, once Taylor leaves the hospital, leaves Brewton, she dies the next morning, before she can sign out a warrant, despite having identified Perry six days earlier, despite telling everyone who asked during the week that he beat her..."

"And somehow forgot when Taylor asked her."

"Right, right, then it becomes a homicide case. Without a warrant for the assault, that's the only charge they could've brought. But Shoffeitt tells Scotty, Taylor, and Henderson in a late night meeting in Mobile on the 13th that she died of natural causes, writes in his report dated the 24th that he can't say how she got her injuries, leaving it to local and state investigators, who aren't investigating an assault, turning over his report to them on the 27th, and the next day I&I reports that no charges have been filed in the case—after Shoffeitt's report says there was no homicide—that they're leaving it up to the grand jury. The grand jury couldn't have done anything with the case, couldn't have indicted anybody, since there was no charge. Even Billy said so. It's like they went through all the motions, knowing they could make the case disappear."

She thought a moment, choosing her words carefully, it turned out, before saying, "How lucky were they that she died?"

"Do you honestly think it was luck?"

She didn't answer, didn't really need to; just gave me a stern, almost preemptive look.

When we got back we found out that Tropical Storm Chris had disappeared too, had fizzled out in the Caribbean, leaving in its wake some rain, some downed tree limbs, perhaps, but no real damage, and no revelations.

Murder Creek

All the Way to the F. B. I.

I LOVE QUOTING that line, the one Hannibal whispers to Clarisse through the bars and Plexiglas of his cell, "...all the way to the F. B. I...." Our "expert" was a former FBI crime scene specialist. We were waiting on his comments about the forensics reports I'd sent him.

"Did you send him the ABI report, too?" Suzanne had asked.

"No. Not yet."

"Why not?"

"Couple of reasons. One, I'm hoping for a quick, professional answer."

"Professional?"

"Yeah, you know, see if he comes up with the same questions we did. Plus, I didn't want to send him any more than he agreed to look at. He'll probably want to see more, though, don't you think?"

"I don't know, and don't know the guy. Ask Jennifer."

Jennifer, Suzanne's daughter-in-law, is the reason we got to this "guy" at all. How that happened is one of those serendipitous circumstances, those happy accidents, which, once they start accumulating—running into Buddy Mitchell at the Archives felt like another one, or meeting Mary Tucker in Monroeville—makes me really believe in a story. There's no other way to explain it. On the other hand, it's as simple and as complex as this: Jennifer meets people. Period.

"How did you happen to hook up with this guy?" I asked her.

"We just met," she said, not even absolutely sure of where, or when, at this point. In an airport; at a bar. "We just met. I was telling him the story…"

"And?"

And, he seemed interested, or curious. They exchanged emails, he said he would look at the report. The guy'd been on some big cases, huge cases, cases anyone would recognize. "He's the Tiger Woods of crime scene investigators," she said.

So I sent him the report.

In the meantime, I combed back through the ABI records and listed every name mentioned on a separate notepad. I intended to ask Suzanne's dad Gene about each of them, about any little thing he might remember of them.

Turned out to be precious little. He recognized the DJ who worked at the radio station, would later own it after the Gardners. He remembered Albert Jackson as a night watchman at the mill, and a nurse who was married to one of his supervisors at T. R. Miller. Beyond that, the other thirty or so names listed sparked no real memories at all. Only a couple of others were even vaguely recognizable to him.

"Not much help," he said.

"Probably wouldn't have had much cause to know these folks."

"No, probably not."

They were part of another Brewton, shadowy ghosts who sifted through the cracks of raising a family, shifting state politics, and national turmoil. They lived and operated on the fringes, the periphery, or worse. They were in another universe, that other America Harrington wrote about: "the real explanation of why the poor are where they are, is that they made the mistake of being born to the wrong parents, in the wrong section of the country, in the wrong industry, or in the wrong racial or ethnic group."[43] In the wrong state, we might add. Certainly on the wrong side of Murder Creek.

But it's easy enough to see how they could get lost in the shuffle of the times. It was a transitional year, 1966, a year when real, wholesale change—if not progress—still seemed tangible after the remarkable initiatives of the previous few years. It was also a year when—true to Emerson's cautioning more than a century earlier—those possibilities seemed to slip through our fingers. 1963 can be taken as the year when those possibilities were set into play, a year that challenged most of our notions about social fabric and responsibility, starting, perhaps, with Martin Luther King's elegiac letter from a Birmingham jail, where he admonished detractors that there was no "inside" and "outside" when it came to justice, saying, "injustice anywhere is a threat to justice everywhere," and "We are caught in an inescapable network of mutuality, tied in a single garment of destiny. Whatever affects one directly, affects all indirectly."[44] The fate of the "more perfect union" itself was in jeopardy just as it was a century earlier. The truth of that sentiment played out nationally throughout the summer. In June, Wallace made his infamous schoolhouse stand at the University of Alabama, leading the state's "shameless defiance of court-ordered school desegregation," what Leslie Dunbar has called the South's second attempt to "shatter the union."[45] Kennedy's federal marshals were called in to remove the obstacle, and the president made his most impassioned speech about the moral crisis the country was in. Shortly afterward, Medgar Evers was assassinated in Jackson, Mississippi, further illustrating the depth of the crisis and the character of the resistance, much as the bombing of Birmingham's Sixteenth Street church just weeks after King's "I Have a Dream" speech did. If that weren't enough, Kennedy's assassination that fall showed the nation and the world what was truly at stake.

Murder Creek

And then change came, or at least a blueprint for change. Taking up JFK's unfinished business, Johnson both pushed through the Civil Rights Act and declared an "unconditional war" on poverty as part of his strategy to complete what FDR had started, the Great Society he campaigned on. Harrington, who was part of the task force drawing up the battle plan for this war, said, "The important thing was not just that the president was going to commit money to the war on poverty. More than that, the enormous moral and political power which the White House can summon was channeled into this undertaking. There was a sense of excitement, of social passion, in the capital."[46] Both initiatives, though primarily the former (together with the following year's Voting Rights Act) cost LBJ and the Democratic Party the South, to this day. And, just like today, Johnson would squander a hard-won, but battle-tested, ready and willing coalition by channeling the "moral and political energy of Washington" that excited Harrington so much—"as well as tens of billions of dollars"—not "into the right war at home," but into a military misadventure half a world away, "the wrong war in Southeast Asia,"[47] escalating involvement in Vietnam to a quarter of a million troops by the fall of 1966, what would ultimately cost him the presidency.

And what was the price of that? Specifically, at least, the war on poverty, though some think much, much more. J. William Fulbright, writing in 1966, said, "America is now at the historical point at which a great nation is in danger of losing its perspective of what exactly is within the realm of its power and what is beyond it. Other great nations reaching this critical juncture, have aspired to too much and, by over extension of effort, have declined and then fallen. Gradually but unmistakably America is showing signs of that arrogance of power which has afflicted, weakened, and in some cases destroyed great nations in the past," a consequence, he said, of confusing "power with virtue."[48] At least one commentator thinks Fulbright's pause is just as applicable today. Charles Bussey is on record, "wish[ing] President

Bush would take a few moments to read Fulbright's book."⁴⁹ Because, as he says, "let there be no mistake, military violence abroad is intimately connected to domestic policies and especially those related to poverty. A wise man once said, 'there is a connection between war and poverty. ... Poverty is militarism's twin.' This administration is using the Iraq misadventure to cloak its war on social programs at home. Instead of LBJ's 'war on poverty,' we seem now to be engaged in a war on the poor."⁵⁰ It wouldn't be too difficult to connect those two dots with the threads of the consequences of Johnson's social initiatives, subsequently "losing the South," Barry Goldwater, etc., but not here.

After King was assassinated in the midst of his Poor People's Campaign, and then Bobby Kennedy—whose funeral train carried "the finest hopes of the decade along with the body of the dead Senator"*—Richard Nixon unaccountably (though predictably) "told the people that the Federal Government had tried to do too much and that he would therefore decentralize social programs and set more modest goals," the "Government was too active," he thought, and "efforts must be cut back and turned over to the states."⁵¹ For Alabama's poor, that was the worst thing that could happen. Their government, after all, in a tragic reversal of Fulbright's cautionary equation, had stolen power† under the

---

* Harrington additionally said of the procession, "It passed through the other America because the affluent never live in sight of the tracks but the poor do," just as in Brewton. "And those tens of thousands standing there—sometimes singing, sometimes saluting, sometimes simply present, silent –were mourning their own aspirations along with the man who had spoken for them." (p. 205.)

† "For years," Harvey Jackson writes in *A Century of Controversy*, "historians have played with the figures, calculated and recalculated to determine if the

guise of virtue. By 1966 there had already been five separate and serious attempts to address the inequities written into the 1901 constitution, every one of them thwarted or ignored by brokers who knew their power lay within its edicts.

There was, however, one breakthrough, one cause for hope for the future. Hope, the "luxury of hope," as Harrington called it, is the one commodity most lacking and most necessary, in the life of the poor. Or as Cornel West says, "the tragicomic commitment to hope," a "mighty shield and inner strength" that sustains the oppressed and the poor, "even while staring in the face of hate and hypocrisy," is one of three necessary "crucial traditions" that "fuel deep democratic energies" combating what he calls "antidemocratic dogmas."[52] Hope is the final refusal to give up.

In an "Afterword" added to the re-issued edition of The Other America, an "overview of the past two decades" since the original publication of the book, Harrington feared that as the twenty year anniversary of Johnson's war approached there were more Americans living in poverty than at the time of the president's declaration, that poverty was still the major, and perhaps even worsening problem facing the country. The essay, he said, is "an analysis of the interrelationships between poverty and the economy and the political movements in the United States", an examination of the definition of poverty, and "a brief review of the programs," past and potential, that "could actually eliminate poverty in the United States."

In discussing these issues it will be necessary to use statistics and other abstractions of economic and social analysis. This has to be done, not the least because there are many people who charge that those of us who speak passionately about the crime of

---

constitution of 1901 was legally ratified. The answer has always been the same." No. (p. 30.)

poverty do so with much heart and little head. ... In a sense, then, those of us who see the misery of the poor as one of the great challenges to our society must prove our case in a "professional," unemotional way.

"But," he then cautioned, "after all the statistics are in, the reader is advised" to spend some time in any city, to "open the eyes, not to the 'data' but to the pinched and hopeless faces of men and women and children forced to live under intolerable conditions."[53] When poverty and hopelessness mounts, he argued, "there is also an increase in social pathology: in alcoholism, drug addiction, family breakdown, and crime."[54]*

Hope, in Alabama, came in the form of the revised judicial article of the constitution, what Robert Martin Schaefer called "A Taste of Reform." In 1966, Howell Heflin, who would go on to become chief justice of the Alabama Supreme Court, and then Senator, commissioned the Citizens Conference on the Alabama Courts. It was a wide ranging coalition of lawyers, businessmen, minorities, and others seeking to reform the state's justice system, which was considered at the time one of the worst in the country. According to Schaefer, the commission was "animated by the judicial branch's lack of professionalism."[55] More specifically, the rule of law in Alabama was nowhere to be found up to that point. For sixty-five years, the Big Mules and the planters controlled the legislature and, in turn, arbitrarily dictated judicial rules of procedure. The will of these legislators, the "ill humors" of these calculating men—the very thing Publius warned against, as quoted by Alexander Hamilton, when he argued for a "truly

---

* That he speaks with authority on this issue is evidenced by the fact that *The Other America*, according to Arthur Schlesinger, in his history of the Kennedy administration, "was a factor in making the President decide that poverty had to become an issue."

distinct" judiciary: "there is no liberty, if the power of judging be not separated from the legislative and executive powers"[56]—trumped the rule of law. As a result, "The civil rights of blacks and poor whites were trampled on with impunity."[57] Schaefer explained just how calculating they were:

> To properly comprehend the issues surrounding the Alabama Constitution today, and the judicial branch in particular, one needs to appreciate that the framers of the 1901 document were concerned with the rule of law. For them it was a precious thing, but only for themselves. Law is necessary because human beings are imperfect. Consequently, the rule of law replaces despotism. Politicians do not simply rule in the United States; rather, laws are supreme. The writers of the 1901 constitution openly spoke of their disdain at having to fraudulently alter ballot boxes to ensure white supremacy. During the convention it was pointed out that the children of the current leaders might imitate their fathers' tendency to break the law. The children were learning to disregard the law. The rule of law, it was argued, was necessary for the preservation of order and protection of property. Ironically, the 1901 delegates insisted that one more election needed to be stolen to guarantee white supremacy. Then the law could be paramount.[58]

This is what convention president Knox was referring to, unwittingly or not, when he said in his opening address, "if we would have white supremacy, we must establish it by law—not by force or fraud. If you teach your boy that it is right to buy a vote, it is an easy step for him to learn to use money to bribe or corrupt officials or trustees of any class. If you teach your boy that it is right to steal votes, it is an easy step for him to believe that it is right to steal whatever he may need or greatly desire." After acknowledging such behavior in the past—"The justification for whatever manipulation of the ballot that has occurred in this State has been the menace of negro domination"—Knox admonished the delegates, saying, "The time comes, when, if they would be free, happy and contented people, they must return to a Constitutional form of government, where law and order prevail, and where every citizen stands ready to stake his life and his honor to maintain it."[59] Of course, that time wouldn't necessarily come until some time after the fraudulent ratification process. Those delegates then placed virtually all control of that "law and order" into the hands of the big-moneyed interests of the state, who then resisted all attempts at reforming the flawed fundamental document of Alabama for sixty-five years. Only through Howell Heflin's 1966 initiative, and seven years worth of work on the part of his commission, was Alabama's judiciary transformed into the respectable body that it is today. Obviously, that reform came too late for Annie Jean. She appeared to have been victimized by the courts' infamous "home cooking," what Schaefer referred to as "a euphemism for the arbitrary justice dished out to nonlocals,"[60] and even near-locals, if you happened to live in East Brewton.

Just as a test—though I'm not entirely sure of exactly what—I retrieved the list of potential grand jurors that was published in the Standard that fall, showed those names to Gene, asked how many of them he recognized. That he could, indeed, identify a vast majority of the seventy names, seemed to say something. Not about Gene as much as about Brewton, and perhaps America, that there is an other America, maybe always has been, that we only glimpse from time to time, as during the depression, or in the sixties, or in the aftermath of a tragedy such as hurricane Katrina. The question becomes, are we making progress toward that grand constitutional principle—its first principle, really—of "forming a more perfect union," or are we haltingly retreating from the responsibility and challenge those founders hoped for?

Murder Creek

We didn't hear back from District Attorney Billy for weeks. And any attempts to contact him went unanswered. A pattern developed in other attempts to talk to those principals whispered to have been involved but who never showed up on the official investigators' witness list.

I sent a letter to Deputy Sheriff James Taylor, who, former residents said, drove Sheriff Byrne everywhere he went. The hunch was that if, according to Willie Mae, Scotty was at the camp house that Sunday morning, Sheriff Taylor would have been there, too. The letter—like all the others, detailing exactly what we were doing—as well as phone calls to his home, were not answered.

We called Mrs. Tom Gardner, Juliana, to confirm the story about the threats to the newspaper and radio if they continued their investigation. The story went that Tom and Juliana were over at Wes Gardner's—the owner of the radio station—home one evening, when an official but unfamiliar car pulled into the drive and two men got out. The children were summoned from playing and taken to their rooms. Their doors, as well as an intermediate door—one that was never closed—pulled to. Children, being children, aware that something not quite usual was going on, listened as best they could. The daughter remembers one of the men telling the journalists to "drop it," and remembers the debate between the adults afterward being decided by the fact that they all had "children to think about." Juliana remembered two members of "law enforcement" coming to the house, but not much else. She said the whole episode was "very upsetting," but that she didn't remember anything else about it.

I called Hugh Caffey and asked him if he'd be willing to talk about the case. Mr. Caffey was the lawyer many of the town's elite went to, it's said, and, was a close associate—though from a distance—of Scotty Byrne's. He, too, said he "didn't really recollect" much about the story. He said he remembered being surprised that nothing ever came of it, said it sure looked like "they were going to drop the hammer" on Perry, but didn't. When I asked him why he thought that was so, he said he didn't know. "You should ask Scotty."

He was interested in how his name came up.

"When I talked to Ralph Barnes," I said, "he mentioned your name."

"Who?"

"Annie Jean's oldest child, Ralph. He said he came to you some time after her death to ask you about it and that you advised him to just leave it alone."

"I said what?" he asked, his tone noticeably shifting.

("I'm surprised he didn't hang up on you right there," a relative told me later.)

But he remained pleasant enough. He didn't remember ever saying that to Ralph, and didn't, moreover, think he could be much help at all with the story. He would be willing to meet, but, "I think it'd be a waste of your time," a wasted trip to his home in the Florida panhandle, where he has since passed away.

We were told a prominent preacher at the time was approached by "the men" involved, seeking counseling. The story originated from the preacher's ex-wife. A call to his home yielded pretty much the same results. Both the preacher and his current wife said they didn't remember anything about the case.

"But it's an instantaneous response," said a friend who was helping us track down the phone numbers, making some of the initial calls. "They're not taking any time to think about it."

And then we were told about a nurse who wanted to talk to Suzanne. The woman had approached that same friend some time after Temple came out, overhearing a discussion of the book, and asked, "Do you know Suzanne Hudson?" She said she had been on duty that day they brought Annie Jean to the hospital, spoke of the horrific condition she was in, and the equally horrified reaction on the part of other nurses and doctors, trained, professional medical personnel, who had to sit, gather themselves, taking it all in. We'd already heard that story, about how repulsed the hospital workers were that day, from a woman who'd been a patient at the time. She told us it was all the doctors and nurses could talk about. This nurse had hinted at something darker, and far more sinister. "Tell Suzanne I have to talk to her."

"She didn't think Annie Jean died of 'natural' causes," the friend said.

"Really?"

"Really. Even sounded to me like she was implicating a doctor."

"You're kidding."

Problem was we didn't have a name.

"I'm sorry. I just can't remember. Didn't I send it to you?" she asked Suzanne. "Maybe there are some folks who might be able to tell us who was working the ER back then. I might remember if I heard it."

"Who?" Suzanne asked.

"Folks Scotty and them would never suspect talking, 'domestics,' like the bartender at the country club," she said, trading a knowing glance with Suzanne. "A maid for the Millers: he'd never believe they'd talk."

"Why's that?" I asked.

"Nothing's changed in Brewton but the Pizza Huts," Suzanne said. "Remember?"

Murder Creek

We went back to Brewton to talk to those folks, but they too either didn't know, or wouldn't say. I wasn't sure which, and wondered out loud, "How is it that so many people keep saying they don't really remember anything about the case?" They remember the event, but nothing, it seemed, beyond that, as if it was perfectly fine that there never was any resolution. "Indifference?"

"No. Couldn't be. These are good people," Suzanne reasoned.

"Then what? Old age?"

"They remembered other things about those years."

Indeed, had vivid memories about segregation, for instance, in those final years of official Jim Crow, the separate accommodations at restaurants and bus stations, areas of town. But what we heard again and again was that Brewton was a good place, and everybody got along, mostly, the people they worked for helped them out. They didn't have the trouble other Alabama cities had.

"You know these people," I said. "Are they scared?"

"Of what, George Perry?"

"What do you mean?"

"What reason would they have to keep quiet if it was just Perry?"

"None that I can think of. But maybe we're trying too hard, looking for answers to questions that just aren't there," I said. "What if it was just Perry? Nothing particularly memorable about a sordid affair gone bad, especially forty years later."

"Then why was he never arrested?"

"I don't know," I confessed.

"And what about the kids?"

Murder Creek

Again, I didn't know.

"The questions are there," she reminded me.

And then I got a message from our expert. "Not much to go on," he wrote of the report. "Feel free to call me." After what felt to me like a roller coaster, I was about ready to give up, get off the damn thing, and drag my sorry ass home, beaten.

"Amazing"

THAT WAS HOW he reacted when I filled him in some more on the story, once I did relent, and call. "Amazing," that no one was arrested. "Amazing," when I told him no one was ever indicted in the case. And when I told him specifically that Perry was the coroner at the time, he said it was "obvious he paid off the toxicologist."

When I asked him how he could tell that, he said it was apparent in the way the report read. "But," he added, "I'm probably not the best person for you to talk to. It's not really my field of expertise." His area was crime scenes, blood splatter, to be exact. "You need to consult a pathologist," he said.

So I called an old friend, a former pathologist, and mailed him the report, again, without elaborating on the case.

"They're trying to protect him," he said, when he called me back.

"Who?"

"The doc."

"Perry?"

"Yeah. You can tell by the way it's worded, that guy, Shoffiet? He's working pretty hard to give a certain slant to the thing."

"Like what?"

"That clot is most suspicious. He mentions it, but then dismisses it."

"That bothered me, too. What do you make of it?"

"Being on the right side, it might have been caused by injecting of a column of air, and stasis. When the air reaches the heart, it stops. Blood already in the chamber pools, and clots."

"How long would something like that take?"

"I don't know, exactly, but it's pretty quick."

"Three minutes?" I asked, the length of time Annie Jean's mother said she was away from her bedside that morning.

"Possibly. But you know who we could probably talk to," he said. "Bucky Phillipi. Remember him?"

Yes, I did, from his residency days at a hospital in Mobile.

"He's the chief pathologist for the Rush group over in Meridian," Mississippi, and he's the son of the other doctor copied on Shoffiet's report. Bucky's from Brewton. His father had partnered with Strandell.

But Bucky wasn't so convinced when I talked with him about the report. He, like the FBI expert, found it lacking in information.

"It says there's microscopic evidence of kidney damage, but none of the actual microscopic findings, and not much in the gross description to support that conclusion."

He wondered out loud why a toxicologist would have performed the autopsy. "Is that the way they did it back then?"

I didn't know, but said that Perry being the coroner—who would have been precluded from those duties in this case—might explain the situation. "I did see one newspaper article that said the sheriff and the DA requested Shoffiet perform the autopsy. Exactly what that means, procedurally, I'm not sure."

Then he said something startling: "Her injuries didn't seem that severe to me. In fact, she probably wouldn't even be admitted to a hospital with those injuries by today's standards."

"Then what do you think happened?"

"Tough to say. The autopsy certainly doesn't explain her death. Unexplained deaths do happen," he said. "But rarely in a hospital. You'd have to have her medical record to really tell."

"We've been told they were destroyed in a fire."

He, like everyone else so far, didn't remember any such fire.

"Feels like we're going around in circles," Suzanne said.

"I know what you mean. I swear, when he said they probably wouldn't even put her in the hospital today, it sounded to me just like Perry telling that Montgomery reporter there was 'nothing wrong with her' when he saw Annie Jean that Sunday morning."

"Oh man," the former pathologist said when he heard the comment, "what would you call that, straddling?"

"At best. It's out of variance with everything else, at the very least."

"He probably has to be careful, being from Brewton," he said. "Clearly, she was beaten, and somebody covered it up," no more able to reconcile the discrepancy than I. "Still, though, Sutton's Law applies."

Or it ought to. Willie Sutton famously responded to the question of why he kept robbing banks, "Because that's where the money is." Such simple logic, taught as a guiding principle to medical students under the guise of Occam's Razor, suggests that if something is crushingly obvious, it's probably worth noticing. The problem is that Annie Jean's case seems to escape that application at every turn.

And that difficulty brought on a kind of inertia, from the silence, from the unwillingness to talk, and the willful forgetfulness. There is no doubt these people are, for the most part, good people, in a town they like to think is a good town, as would anyone. The question becomes how jeopardized is that comfortable illusion by uncomfortable truth? Where exactly is the line between not knowing, not wanting to know, and keeping secrets? And don't they realize that it is all, essentially, the same burden?

Passing on an opportunity to serve justice, to preserve the rule of law, just because it challenges your accustomed comfort zone is tantamount to abdicating democratic responsibility. It is at least, perhaps, exhibiting an indifference to individual democratic responsibility we can hardly afford these days, if we ever could. "The greatest threats" to our democracy, Cornel West writes in Democracy Matters, is "the rise of three dominating antidemocratic dogmas. These three dogmas, promoted by the most powerful forces in our world, are rendering American democracy vacuous."[61] The counter to this vacuousness, the opposition to the forces bankrupting our democracy, emptying it of its promise, West says, is "to reconnect with the energies of a deep democratic tradition in America and reignite them."[62] Those energies are likewise threefold: "The first is the Greek creation of the Socratic commitment to questioning—questioning of ourselves, of authority, of dogma, of parochialism, and of fundamentalism." The second is "the Jewish invention of the prophetic commitment to justice—for all peoples." And the third is the "tragicomic commitment to hope."[63] These are all, first and foremost, energies located within and fueled by each individual citizen in a democracy. "The first grand democratic experiment in Athens was driven," West reminds us, "by a movement of the demos—citizen-peasants—organizing to make the Greek oligarchs who were abusing their power accountable. Democracy is always a movement of an energized public to make elites responsible—it is at its core and most basic foundation the taking back of one's powers in the face of the misuse of elite power."[64] What, can reasonably be asked, is the opposite? What happens to democracy, to society, when good—or at least well-intended—

people refuse a chance to take a stand for justice? Not everyone can be expected, or even knows how to be an activist, of course, but when given a chance, a choice, they must act on it. Shouldn't they?

"In the face of elite manipulations and lies, we must draw on the Socratic," West challenges, "a relentless self-examination and critique of institutions of authority, motivated by an endless quest for intellectual integrity and moral consistency," an attempt, moreover, to awaken "people from their uncritical sleepwalking."[65]

Drawing on the rhetorical model of Martin Luther King, Jr., in his efforts to change society by appealing to one heart and soul at a time, West continues: "In the face of callous indifference to the suffering wrought by our imperialism, we must draw on the prophetic." He is addressing, in this passage, larger national and international matters, but the message applies, nonetheless, to local matters, individual matters. Because "[t]he Jewish invention of the prophetic commitment to justice ... one of the great moral moments in human history ... consists of human acts of justice and kindness that attend to the unjust sources of human hurt and misery. Prophetic witness calls attention to the causes of unjustified suffering and unnecessary social misery. It highlights personal and institutional evil, including especially the evil of being indifferent to personal and institutional evil."[66]

Lastly, he says, "In the face of cynical and disillusioned acquiescence to the status quo, we must draw on the tragicomic. Tragicomic hope is a profound attitude toward life reflected in the work of artistic geniuses as diverse as Lucian in the Roman empire, Cervantes in the Spanish empire, and Chekhov in the Russian empire. Within the American empire it has been most powerfully expressed in the black invention of the blues in the face of white supremacists power." He then quotes Ralph Ellison explaining, "The blues is an impulse to keep the painful details and episodes of a brutal experience alive in one's aching consciousness, to finger its jagged grain, and transcend it, not by the consolation of philosophy but by squeezing from it a near-tragic, near-comic lyricism."[67]

Is this what Joyce, Brenda, Ralph, George Jr., and the rest are doing—to particularize West's argument—fanning these deep democratic energies by keeping the "painful details" of this episode alive, questioning elite entitlement and authority or employing others to question for them, in an attempt to highlight personal evil? I don't know that they'd say that, explicitly, but if it is true that "there is a deep public reverence for—a love of—democracy in America and a deep democratic tradition, ... [a] profound democratic impulse that stretches all the way back to the Greeks,"[68] those energies are implicit in their search for truth and justice. As such, if it is also true that we're encountering, at any point along this quest, willful forgetfulness, refusal to remember, an indifference to any apparent personal evil, then there's more at stake then the reputation of those involved or the city of Brewton in general.

If the "high point of the black response to American terrorism" occurred when Emmett Till's mother declared from the lectern during her son's funeral, "I don't have a minute to hate. I'll pursue justice for the rest of my life,"[69] the parallel can be drawn, then, to anyone who makes the same choice, takes up the same pursuit. At the very least, I think, however it came about that those five children of Annie Jean's showed up at the Brewton Public Library that evening in September of 2003, it is not too much of a stretch to suppose that part of the impulse which drove them to attend Suzanne's reading stemmed from a similar desire to see justice served.

So What?

I WONDERED OUT loud, about the story, regardless of the parallels I thought I saw in this quest with all those other, larger issues. So what if it resonates with West's argument? "If people aren't going to be moved by what he's saying," I complained, reading passages of the book, where nearly every word thundered off the page. But then, I'd felt the same power and urgency in the work of David Brock, even, oddly enough, Al Franken. "This is, at bottom, and in all honesty, a local story."

"I don't agree," Suzanne insisted. "What did Baldwin say?"

I'd read her a passage from his essay, "The Creative Process," fondly rediscovered in West's book:

The artist cannot and must not take anything for granted, but must drive to the heart of every answer and expose the question the answer hides.

We know, in the case of the person, that whoever cannot tell himself the truth about his past is trapped in it, is immobilized in the prison of his undiscovered self. This is also true of nations.[70]

"Dare tell me..." she started; another quote.

This one was from Lillian Smith, fierce anti-segregation activist, the author who wrote Strange Fruit. "...dare tell me you have the strength to combat what you find..." is the inscription chosen for Where We Stand.*

"What you find," Suzanne insisted.

---

* And, in another of those curiosities I probably, in all honesty, pay *too* much attention to, Lillian Smith died four days after Annie Jean.

"I get it, I get it."

We were returning from Brewton yet again, having attended Suzanne's high school reunion, driving south, stopping for tacos in Bay Minette. We'd gone, mostly, to get reactions from her classmates and friends about the story, as they remembered it then, or what they thought about it now. I'd been mostly disappointed by their reactions, which is what prompted my sullen, "So what?" The festivities themselves, though, had been more interesting.

We arrived in Brewton early that Friday afternoon, leaving Fairhope as soon as we could get away from work. We got there a little too late to make it out to the staging area for the parade out at the high school, and waited for the procession by the Methodist Church on Belleville Avenue. There, Suzanne ran along side and finally hopped up onto the fire truck carrying her class. I made my way downtown to claim a spot along the curb outside Willie's restaurant amongst the throngs of school kids and adults decked out in their T. R. Miller red, holding plastic grocery sacks, waiting for the candy and footballs and beads the revelers would throw into the crowd as they rolled by.

I met an elderly woman there on the sidewalk, Pearl Stallworth, who was attracted by the t-shirt I was wearing, a Negro League Hall of Fame shirt. "You don't see many white men wearing a shirt like that in Brewton," she said.

I told her why I was there, said I was writing a book about Brewton, which prompted her to relate her own tale about murder and justice and retribution in Brewton. Turns out she'd had three sons killed in town a few years earlier. The shooter was caught, convicted, and imprisoned. Pearl petitioned the then governor, and a memorial park was built on the site. She works near there now for a children's hospice and advocacy group.

Once the parade was over, the football team filed by us on the sidewalk on their way to their pre-game meal in Willie's. She interrupted our chat to jostle with the players, challenge their spirit and offer encouragement.

"Hey, hey," she said to one, then another. "Where's the noise, where's the juice?" she called. And when they seemed not to recognize her, added, "You know me," looking up into their eyes.

"Yeah, yeah," one of them answered, pumping a fist for the battle to come.

"That's what I'm talking about," she said, then to me, "I worked custodial at the school for years."

She gave me her card, invited me to call, hinted, "I know all about Brewton."

Everyone I met over the next few hours at a reception for the alumnus, at the football stadium, was equally responsive to the idea of a book about Brewton, and most of them even remembered the "incident," though none had anything by way of specific memories. It was more of the same: they were aware of how upset the town was, but couldn't offer any details.

"Wish I'd listened closer," one told me.

The idea was to mingle within the assembly, talk about Brewton, the case, try to get a sense for how it affected their opinions of the city, if at all. Most of that effort was lost to catching up on time past, retelling old stories, and trying to put names to faces grown less familiar with age. And then once at the stadium, all was forgotten, and forgiven, as the true pride of Brewton took the field, the T. R. Miller tigers.

I remember asking a couple of times, "Who are they playing?"

Murder Creek

No one seemed to know. No one seemed to care. And I admit I got swept into that communal civic fervor once seated on the cold, hard concrete steps that served as stands.

It was a perfect evening for high school football, just as I'd like to think it had been a perfect high school football evening that Friday night in September, 1966. I couldn't help but think about Ralph, and that evening forty years ago, in the midst of the hoopla and buzz, the pageantry, really, of a high school football game. There's no reason to think he wasn't just as excited and animated as the teenagers I spotted roaming the stadium, too cool to sit with parents or grown-ups, too full of energizing promise to sit at all. And there's plenty of reason to wonder how drastically his life was changed shortly after that football game, how much of that energy was sapped out of his spirit, and why.

South Alabama had had its first cold snap that week, the middle of October. Folks were bundled in sweaters and jackets, welcoming the body heat generated by the overflow crowd in the stadium, where the previous five Friday nights they would have been sweating side-by-side waiting for the blistering sun to go down. Not this night.

The section reserved for returning alumni, situated to the right of the elevated press box on the westward facing host stands, was partitioned out for six different graduating classes, dating back forty-five years, oldest to most recent, as the steps rose into the night sky. Across the façade of the press box was a banner emblazoned with the six different state championships the team had won. Suzanne pointed out people she recognized in the class of 1966 below us, "There's Scotty's son." I looked for Buddy Mitchell, and George Jr., who would have been in the same class. As part of the special occasion—it was homecoming weekend as well—the combined middle school and high school marching bands took the field to play "Amazing Grace" and the "National Anthem" before play began. I heard someone off my left shoulder say, "This is how we circumvent the school prayer ban at T. R. Miller," as the opening strains echoed over the field. I couldn't tell if the remark was motivated by pride or cynicism, and not just a stab at humor, and actually wanted to believe the former. It was that beautiful a night, the last traces of dusk bleeding from the sky beyond the visiting stands opposite where we stood. And by the time those in the stands who were singing along had finished drawing out, "And the home, of the, brave..." that sky had become a cool, slate grey curtain beyond the bright lights raised high above the turf.

Then all attention turned to the action within that illumination, all shades of any distinction dissipated for forty-eight minutes of unshakable allegiance. Young, old, black, white, rich, poor: none of that mattered, not even in Brewton, as everyone—the black women who had been part of the first integrated class at Miller, the rich descendent of the city's wealthiest elite, rednecks, children, teenagers, everyone—cheered their hometown team. I wondered, though, if those twelve, fourteen Friday nights each year was a sufficient enough distraction from harsher realities. Except, I remembered, they probably don't ask those questions.

"That's why nothing ever changes," I said on that ride back to Fairhope.

"Why's that?"

"They don't question, don't challenge. Why would the questions themselves be threatening?"

"You think they want change?"

"Some must."

"You saw them last night."

"Yes, I did."

I'd been thinking about it. At the heart of Suzanne's insistent—and only half-joking—claim that "nothing's changed but the Pizza

Huts," is a bitter truth probably best articulated by James Baldwin, not surprisingly. Writing, in part, to his nephew, on the occasion of the centennial of the Emancipation Proclamation, on the eve of the second Reconstruction of the South, he said:

> Perhaps the whole root of our trouble, the human trouble, is that we will sacrifice all the beauty of our lives, will imprison ourselves in totems, taboos, crosses, blood sacrifices, steeples, mosques, races, armies, flags, nations, in order to deny the fact of death, which is the only fact we have. It seems to me that one ought to rejoice in the fact of death—ought to decide, indeed, to earn one's death by confronting with passion the conundrum of life. One is responsible to life: it is the small beacon in that terrifying darkness from which we come and to which we shall return. One must negotiate this passage as nobly as possible, for the sake of those who are coming after us. ... It is the responsibility of free men to trust and to celebrate what is constant—birth, struggle, and death are constant, and so is love, though we may not always think so—and to apprehend the nature of change, to be able and willing to change. I speak of change not on the surface but in the depths—change in the sense of renewal. But renewal becomes impossible if one supposes things to be constant that are not—safety, for example, or money, or power. One clings then to chimeras, by which one can only be betrayed, and the entire hope—the entire possibility—of freedom disappears.[71]

"But don't they know?"

"That's the problem," Suzanne said. "They won't know until it's too late."

"What West is saying."

"Right. 'We must work and hope for such an awakening once again'," she quoted the scholar.

This "awakening" West speaks of and hopes for is "from the seductive lies and comforting illusions that sedate [the populace] and a moral channeling of new political energy that constitutes a formidable threat to the status quo." Because, he says, "we must remember that the basis of democratic leadership is ordinary citizens' desire to take their country back from the hands of corrupted plutocratic and imperial elites."[72] In short, what West is calling for is a populist revolt, not unlike the last great grassroots insurrection of the 1890s. West himself draws a connection between then and now. Such an awakening, in his view, "is what happened in the 1860s, 1890s, 1930s, and 1960s in American history. Just as it looked as if we were about to lose the American democratic experiment—in the face of civil war, imperial greed, economic depression, and racial upheaval—in each of these periods a deep democratic awakening an activistic energy emerged to keep our democratic project afloat."[73] This is what he hopes will "happen again."

That the trajectory of Annie Jean's story traces a similar arc as those movements is no coincidence. The Civil War set the stage and tenor for everything that followed, but is otherwise not a specific consideration here.*

The uprising during what Twain dubbed the "Gilded Age" (quite likely at about the same time he was dissing poor Pollard, Alabama), the "last true grassroots political movement in United States history," was "led by southern and western farmers suffering from a combination of low prices and the inability to

---

* Although it resonates quite clearly with West's argument. John Egerton, in his contribution to *Where We Stand*, says George W. Bush and his administration run "the federal government as you might imagine the Confederates having done if they had won the Civil War. It is almost as if we had come full circle, back to a time of blatant discrimination and arrogant disdain for human rights." (p. 219)

obtain credit on reasonable terms."[74] At a time of unprecedented economic expansion, along with personal prosperity and philanthropy (this is the era of Carnegie's great endowments), the populist revolt was all about money, which was scarce in the post-war South, concentrated and controlled in the Northeast. The efforts of the Farmers Alliance—to create a more accessible currency and credit system, the mining and coining of silver to expand the money supply—was even called by some "the revolt against the East." In order to achieve their desired results—a frightening prospect for the big-time planters, industrialists, bankers and lawyers who controlled the economics of Alabama, known collectively as the "Bourbons"—meant the Populists had to get politically active. Populist gubernatorial candidate Kolb's near-misses in 1890 and 1892 prompted the first post-Reconstruction disfranchisement measure by the state's worried Democrats, with the passage of the Sayre Election Law during the 1892-93 session. It effectively restricted the voting rights of the state's illiterate and semi-literate citizens. Before Sayre, voting ballots were distributed by the political parties, and voters who could not read could tell the candidates apart by color-coding or symbols. Under the new law, ballots were distributed by the state, with candidates listed alphabetically, without colors or symbols designating parties or offices. T. R. Miller, namesake of the school and stadium, patriarch of the town, just building his mill in Brewton in 1892, might not have been able to vote after Sayre, being an illiterate man who couldn't sign his own name.

The 1930s, of course, is when Annie Jean was born, during the height of the Great Depression. More importantly, FDR's New Deal saw, among other things, the creation of a vibrant middle class, the life's blood of any democracy, the only real and true "check" on governmental abuse of power—the "ordinary citizens" Cornel West is appealing to, at the same time other writers are warning of their endangerment. Thom Hartman, *Screwed: The Undeclared Against the Middle Class and What You Can Do About*

It, that the middle class is essential to a workable democracy, and that same middle class is threatened more seriously now than at any other time since FDR.

"Let us not be afraid to help each other," Roosevelt said. "Let us not forget that government is ourselves and not an alien power over us," a sentiment, however inspired and inspiring it was, that lasted little more than a generation, and did not, really, survive the 1960s, with Nixon decentralizing the social programs of the New Deal and the Great Society, a lifespan almost exactly that of Annie Jean Barnes, likewise cut short far too young.

The battle Hartman and others see—dismantling unions, the privatization of social programs—rolls back not just the efforts of FDR and Johnson, it also contradicts the very ideas of what a responsible democracy is, as put forth by Theodore Roosevelt. And it is a battle long lost in Alabama. Its Constitution "enshrined an unfair tax system that afforded certain groups special privileges," a practice that "violated the principle that each should pay according to his means."[75]

It will take no less of an awakening, no less of a grassroots movement, no less of a "formidable threat to the status quo," to correct the wrongs of Alabama's fundamental charter. That there is a growing band of "ordinary citizens" working tirelessly to take their state back from corrupted and imperial elites is encouraging. But the closer they get, the stiffer entrenched opposition—those adherents to the status quo; those, Baldwin might have said, who rely on the constancy of money and power—becomes.

Murder Creek

I Tremble for my Country

"I TREMBLE FOR my country," Thomas Jefferson wrote, considering slavery in his Notes on the State of Virginia, "When I reflect that God is just..." He was writing this before the U.S. constitutional convention, in the early 1780s. It was a much more complex issue. Slavery had been, and would be for the next half-century, bound up in the new nation's economic and foreign policies. There was a clear moral choice: witness Washington's decision to free his slaves after the war. But it was not an easy or uncomplicated one, as Lincoln reiterated some four-score years later.

On May 22, 1901, the Alabama Constitutional Convention was opened with a prayer by the Reverend Dr. Patterson to that same, supposedly just God:

"Oh Lord, God, our Heavenly Father," Dr. Patterson intoned, "we come this morning with prayer to Thee for guidance, for strength and for wisdom and for blessing. ... We pray Thee, Heavenly Father, that Thou wilt cause Thy face to shine upon these Thy servants, who are met together from different parts of this State to engage in this undertaking which is before them, and we ask that Thou will give to them wisdom; that Thou will give to them clearness of mind, and especially that Thou will give to them a sense of the responsibility resting upon them, and as they day by day meet for consultation and deliberation, may their minds and hearts be so guided and controlled by Thy Holy Spirit as that the result of their labors will be of benefit to all the inhabitants and citizens of this State. We pray that Thou wilt restrain them from any unwise proceedings," he continued, before ending his plea, "to Thy name's honor and glory, Amen."[76]

Only moments later, though, during president Knox's address to the convention delegates, the citizens and inhabitants who would actually benefit from their undertaking, and those who would be subjugated to a lesser status because of their undertaking, were defined.

"Then, as now," Knox said immediately after greeting his fellow delegates and thanking them for the honor they'd bestowed upon him, "the negro was the prominent factor in the issue."

By convention's end those "servants" produced a document benefiting mostly themselves, impeding, in fact, all other possibility of progress. As early as 1915, in his departing address to the legislature, Governor Emmet O'Neal indicted the constitution, writing, "Many of the provisions of our present antiquated fundamental law constitute insuperable barriers to most of the important reforms necessary to meet modern conditions and to secure economy and efficiency in the administration of every department of state government."[77]

O'Neal had served on the convention delegation. He had, even, argued for home rule, unsuccessfully. Only after he was elected governor in 1910 did he realize, through experience, how restrictive the constitution was, especially when it came to funding education. "The first and most important step to improve the educational conditions in Alabama," he told the University of Alabama alumni in 1914, "would be the convening of a constitutional Convention to revise our present antiquated fundamental law."[78]

O'Neal's was the first major political voice raised against what had transpired in 1901, though not nearly the last. As of this writing, the voices opposed to reform are gathering and growing louder, stifling those efforts so far, even if, as Wayne Flynt says, their arguments are "couched in appeals to biblical origins and American virtue, neither of which played much of a role in the morally flawed document that had governed Alabama for a century."[79]

Murder Creek

There may have been an American precedent for establishing white supremacy back in 1901, that convention's primary objective, regrettably, but it could hardly be considered a virtue. And if there ever were biblical origins to the document, that would have necessitated a just and compassionate instrument, which it is not. A truly just and compassionate fundamental law, an actual democratically virtuous constitution, would strive toward what Dr. Patterson prayed for back in 1901. It would "benefit all of the inhabitants and citizens" of the state.

Clearly, white supremacy is no longer an official state policy, but it took an embarrassingly long time to purge the vestiges of that purely un-democratic, non-biblical program. Indeed, it wasn't until the autumn of 1966—about the time the grand jury was recessing in Annie Jean's case—in a deal Bob Vance engineered with the state's newly enfranchised black voters, that "White Supremacy" was removed from the state's Democratic Committee emblem. But the document's many other egregious flaws still cry out for correction—notably educational funding, a cry that's gone unheeded for over ninety years. As late as 2001, then Governor Don Siegelman knew Alabama's schools needed fixing, knew that in order to fix the schools the government needed fixing, which meant reforming the constitution.

An organization opposing Siegelman's efforts, the Association for Judeo-Christian Values, equated those efforts with a "national movement to change sex education in schools," which "opens the way for teaching children acceptance of homosexuality," according to the association's executive director, Sandra Lane Smith.[80] Siegelman's executive order established the Alabama Advisory Council for Safe Schools, whose mandate was to decrease school violence, by teaching tolerance, among other things.

At a rally sponsored by Ms. Smith's organization, Kayla Moore, wife of former Alabama Chief Justice Roy Moore, offered her reasons for opposing reform to the dozen or so spectators. "The 100-year-old constitution is not outdated," she said, adding, "The U.S. Constitution is twice as old. And the Bible is thousands of years old." Then, for whatever reason, she witnessed, "Man is inherently evil. The constitution restrains evil,"[81] painting reformers as equally evil, presumably.

Except her husband, in his official capacity as the state's top judge, refused to yield to the constitutional restraint in the establishment clause. He clandestinely erected a monument to the Ten Commandments in the courthouse lobby, and then defied Supreme Court orders to remove it, until he was removed from office instead.

Other spokespersons opposed to reform have reasons for their stance which run from slightly more cogent fears of raised taxes and legalized gambling to hysterical accusations that reformers want to "strip citizen rights from the constitution and remove state boundaries."[82] The rally Mrs. Moore addressed was one of a series of "educational seminars" intended to inform voters on what Ms. Smith and her colleagues believe are the real motives of reformers, going so far to stoke fear in citizens' minds as to suggest that a constitutional rewrite would "pave the way for a United Nations takeover of the state"![83] The tactic is an old, yet ridiculously effective one. The same bogeyman was paraded before voters to push through the 1875 constitution—though dressed up as Northern Reconstructionists—and again in 1901, when conservative Democrats, the Big Mules and the Planters, returned to and then solidified their power, respectively.

J. Michael Allen and Jamison W. Hinds defined the parameters of the debate in a more scholarly fashion for the Alabama Law Review.* They quote Thomas Jefferson in a letter to Samuel

---

* Though, because both are Alabama Law School graduates, their argument

Kercheval dated July 12, 1816, in the epigraph to their article: "I am certainly not an advocate for frequent changes in laws and constitutions. But law and institutions must go hand in hand with the progress of the human mind." They then say, "These words etched in the wall of the Jefferson Memorial in Washington, D.C. describe the plight of Alabama, captured in an ancient constitution that discourages growth, progression, and efficiency," further explaining, "Because it is flawed and unwieldy, Alabama's constitution is an anachronistic impediment to reform and a barrier to efficient state and local government. At the advent of the new millennium, the Legislature should initiate a process of reform to restore faith in state government and prepare Alabama for challenges ahead." But Allen and Hinds are fully cognizant of the principle obstacle to the process: "Because many of the state's special interests are protected by the current document, meaningful reform may be politically unrealistic." And they illustrate the Machiavellian entanglement, quoting from The Prince:

It must be considered that there is nothing more difficult to carry out, nor more doubtful of success, nor more dangerous to handle, than to initiate a new order of things. For the reformer has enemies in all those who profit by the old order, and only lukewarm defenders in all those who would profit by the new order, this lukewarmness arising partly from fear of their adversaries, who have the laws in their favour; and partly from

---

probably falls on deaf ears within the Association for Judeo-Christian Values and its umbrella, Citizens for Responsible Constitutional Reform. They claim that "self-serving lawyers" want to control the rewrite process, inciting an elliptical paranoia that because lawyers dominated the 1901 convention they should somehow be prohibited today.

the incredulity of mankind, who do not truly believe in anything new until they have had actual experience of it.

In the face of such dire analysis, Allen and Hinds still conclude that reform must be pursued for these specific reasons: "Alabama should enact home rule, strengthen the power of the governor, allow counties to devise their own property tax rates, provide for a constitutional revision cycle to prevent the stagnation that currently plagues the document, and eliminate the constitution's excessive 'earmarking' of state funds." [84] In other words, instead of the incomprehensible document bloated by, at last count, over a thousand amendments addressing mostly localized statutory issues, they're calling for a return to a fundamental document that outlines the principle of laws that govern the state. Why this can only be achieved by a rewriting of the constitution is inherent in the 1901 constitution in the first place, especially in those features inherited by the 1875 constitution, the so-called "constitution of prohibition." Those restrictions handcuff local county and municipal authorities from acting on their own, necessitating legislative initiative to grant them the imprimatur to perform their elected—by local citizens—duties; ergo, another amendment. An Alabama Law Institute study found that nearly seventy percent of the amendments affected only one city, one county, or a county and its cities, many of them for school taxes at a very local level. That is, Alabama's controlling document has been amended upwards of some seven hundred times by statutory inclusions that concern, at best, a single county in the state; concerns, quite likely, the other fifty-some counties couldn't care less about. There's absolutely no defending a system where all the state's voters choose if Jefferson County can prohibit suburban prostitution, if Fayette County can raise taxes to hire more firefighters, or whether folks in tiny little White Hall can play bingo. To suggest that the constitution's flaws are best addressed individually, by more amendments,* seems either blithely ignorant of the problem, or hypocritical. Ignorant because the problem is largely one of necessitating amendments to the constitution in order to circumvent the broad prohibitions of the constitution. You don't normally, so far as I know, cure diseases by exacerbating the symptoms. And hypocritical because inevitably, somewhere in those same arguments, you'll find claims that to rewrite the constitution will impede citizens' rights and/or empower government too much, when the paramount objective of reform—one wonders how many times, or how many different ways it has to be said before it registers—is to return local control to local officials, the aforementioned "home rule"—an issue, lest we forget, the South went to war over, a recognition that ought to, really, put an end to the debate. It even seems, moreover, that it's another debate equally reducible by Sutton's Law.

Allen and Hinds readily concede, though, that "without a strong governor to take the lead, Alabama's constitutional reform will likely remain on the drawing board,"[85] in large part, again, because of the constitution itself. Their concern is a legitimate one, especially when considering the list of governors that have tried, but failed, to marshal reform efforts in the past.

In the 1920s, as O'Neal before him, Governor Thomas Kilby likewise found the constitution far too restrictive for responsive and responsible government. He called for a commission to study how it might be rewritten. But also like O'Neal, Kilby saved his condemnation until the end of his term, only delivering it to congress upon his departure. In the next decade two different

---

* As plenty of folks do, such as the president of the Alabama Eagle Forum, another conservative Christian group, like the state's Christian Coalition chapter, completely at odds with statewide religious groups, including the Alabama Baptist Convention, United Methodists, South Alabama Catholics, the Episcopal Diocese of Alabama and the Presbyterian Church.

non-governmental groups called for a new constitution: the Brookings Institute in 1932, and then again by a citizens group called the Alabama Policy Committee in 1938. Neither study resulted in any movement toward reform.

"The most ardent champion for a new constitution," said Bailey Thomson, "proved to be not a business progressive but rather a spiritual heir of populism," Governor James E. Folsom, "Big Jim."

In 1946, Folsom, all six feet, eight inches of him, "campaigned with a string band called the Strawberry Pickers. They would warm up the crowds in school auditoriums or courthouse squares. Then Folsom would take the microphone and, holding up a corn shuck mop, promise to clean out Montgomery. He liked to talk about letting a 'cool, green breeze' blow through the Capitol. In his rustic plain speech, he articulated what many people wanted, as attention shifted to peacetime and hopes for prosperity. He promised to build new roads and provide better schools. Old people would have small pensions, and teachers would earn adequate pay. Above all, Folsom maintained that Citizens should rule and not the plantation owners and industrialists who traditionally ran things in Montgomery." [86]

His victory stunned the political establishment. Folsom was a welcomed new breed of Southern statesman, who did not race bait, and did not blame outside agitators. "Rather, he tried to explain to people that Alabama had inflicted much of the backwardness on itself through its failure to embrace the nation's democratic ideals."[87] And the number one obstacle impeding those people of Alabama, he said, "was the 1901 Alabama Constitution—the source of the ruling elite's power."[88]

"True to his promise, Folsom brought constitutional reform to center stage,"[89] not at the end of his term, like O'Neal and Kilby, but from day one, declaring in his inaugural address, "I am not afraid of too much democracy. I am afraid of what happens to people when they have too little democracy."

Within weeks Folsom had the Legislature in a special session, insisting that it pass a measure for a constitutional convention. "Only through rewriting the state's fundamental charter, he argued, could citizens hope to achieve fair representation in place of the rotten borough system that had prevailed since 1901."[90] His initial efforts, then, became trying to uproot that system, the planter-industrialist coalition that had held sway over government for so long, calling for reapportionment in order to grant proportional representation for more rural areas, the piney woods, the Wiregrass, and the hill country, areas that flank Brewton to the south and the north, populist areas that had revolted against the conservative Democrats in the 1890s. But special interests like the Alabama Farm Bureau, together with "sympathetic" senators in the Legislature, thwarted those efforts.

Prohibited by the constitution from succeeding himself, Folsom returned to office in 1954, popular enough this go around that some senators considered cooperating with him in his renewed crusade for reform. That battle was soon eclipsed by a reinvigorated fight for white supremacy, however, as school desegregation, in the wake of the Brown decision, dominated and polarized the state. A moderate on race and less than prone to resist the push for civil rights, Folsom stood no chance at all in that charged atmosphere.

The best opportunity for reform since 1901 came a decade later, in the fall of 1966, when Albert Brewer won election as lieutenant governor, campaigning, in part, against the same coalition Folsom fought, and for a new constitution. When Governor Lurleen Wallace died of cancer in May of 1968, Brewer ascended to the post, and took every advantage of the position.

He called for a constitutional commission to concentrate on those portions of the 1901 version that most needed reform, principally home rule. In the 1969 Legislative session he used the full weight of his office to direct the congress to draw up a plan for proceeding. But in 1970 those plans were sabotaged by George Wallace. With his sights set on the 1972 presidential election, Wallace double-crossed Brewer in that year's governor's race, first assuring Brewer he wouldn't oppose him, then jumping in anyway. Even so, with many of the state's newspapers supporting Brewer's bid, he beat Wallace in the first primary. "Shocked at what appeared to be a repudiation of his politics, Wallace and his supporters resorted in the second primary to a bagful of dirty tricks so outrageous that even the nation's press took notice. So that no one missed the point, Wallace's campaign newspaper warned that blacks were about to seize control of the state. The appeal to old prejudices worked, thereby ending Brewer's promising career as a reformer."[91]

Bereft of the leadership, support, or even the concern of the renewed chief executive, Brewer's commission pressed on, presenting "its final report on May 1, 1973, along with its proposed revision of the 1901 Constitution," recommending "seven basic principles for reformers to follow."[92] These included loosening restrictions on the legislature and the governor, a call for annual sessions, home rule, and modernizing the judicial article, the last measure the only one to be acted upon, through the efforts of Heflin's committee.

Fob James succeeded Wallace in 1979 and called for the Legislature to make the suggested changes and put it to voters for ratification. The Senate approved his offer, but not the House.

"During his winning 1982 campaign for lieutenant governor, Bill Baxley had stressed the need for constitutional reform, and once in office he moved to make good on his pledge to work for it. George Wallace, now serving his fourth and final term, remained uninterested.

"Baxley named a special committee to draft a new constitution. This group focused on 'cleaning up' the cluttered 1901 document by eliminating obsolete and duplicative provisions, the end result of which would be a constitution shorter by two-thirds and more understandable as well. For the first time, a 'new' constitution did pass both houses of the legislature in 1983." It was not to be, though. Under the prodding of Black Belt Senator Rick Manley, "The Alabama Supreme Court ruled six to three that the Alabama constitution did not permit the legislature to put before the voters a new constitution in the guise of a single amendment to the present document."[93]

Fast forward nearly twenty years, and witness that part of Kayla Moore's condemnation of Governor Don Siegleman's efforts—who actually came to the reform movement late as governor, stinging from the defeat of his lottery proposal designed to generate necessary funds for education and keep some of the revenue crossing the state's borders into lotteries in Tennessee, Georgia, Florida, and Louisiana—which included his involvement in Baxley's failed 1983 reform attempt. The logic goes something like this: because the legislature was then offering a single amendment for ratification by voters (an amendment which would have paved the way for recompiling the unwieldy constitution, a necessary first step toward reforming the thing, as nearly everyone agrees), by only the strictest interpretation that was viewed—arguably—as a violation of the constitution. Ignoring the fact that both chambers of Congress and a third of the Court didn't see it that way, in Mrs. Moore's characterization that meant Siegelman was intent on loosing the restraints of the constitution and allowing "inherently evil" men to run roughshod over the state. She was peddling fear, fear at the expense of truth.

The antidote for fear is hope. At the same time Moore, Smith, the Association for Judeo-Christian Values, the Alabama Eagle Forum, and the rest of them were beating their drums of good and evil, a true grassroots movement was assembling and working toward offering this hope: "a reform movement . . . gathering momentum. And its leaders fully understand the need to generate support both at the top, beginning with the governor, and at the grass roots, where the citizens are."[94] The Alabama Citizens for Constitution Reform operates under the principle that "a modern constitution would speak to citizens' aspirations for their democracy. The U.S. Constitution is the model for the world because it embodies and articulates the belief that free people can govern themselves in a republic. That achievement contrasts with the Alabama Constitution's shameful attempt to roll back democracy and freeze into place conditions that discouraged people from becoming educated, productive citizens."[95] It is an organization comprised of members that cut across all lines. "[A]cross the state, a growing and diverse army of young new leaders is learning to work together for larger causes. They are the nucleus of the rallies and forums now demanding constitutional reform. ... In fact, one would have to go all the way back to the 1890s to find a more fertile time for citizenship. The Populists from that depression-ridden era sent hundreds of speakers into the field, demanding honest elections, fair labor laws and other reforms. They organized study groups to educate citizens. No wonder the Big Mule alliance was determined to bury this movement under the 1901 constitution."[96] Indeed, "Although five governors and a lieutenant governor had advocated constitutional reform and on three occasions their efforts had even inspired proposed new documents, no citizens group had operated independently to build grassroots support for change."[97] The reasons for that are both simple and profoundly critical, for meaningful change, and to this story. "Because [the Constitution] has not been a disaster for everyone. Moreover, in one of the most successful political ploys in the history of a state where voters have been frequently fooled into voting against their own interests, those Big Mules who did well under the constitution have convinced voters that any change would only make things worse." And those voters, "innately conservative and fearful of losing what little they have, believe them."[98]

Or worse. State Representative Demetrius Newton, one of the sponsors of reform initiatives in the most recent legislative session, told David White of The Birmingham News, "Many of our citizens, despite the hard work that this group has done, they're still ignorant in terms of what needs to be done, and even where they are as individuals as it relates to constitutional reform."[99] That group he speaks of, Alabama Citizens for Constitutional Reform, is waging its campaign against both those impediments, trying to overcome generations of distrust amongst voters, and at the same time trying to educate them about the stakes. Both are challenging tasks. The latter is a challenge of logistics and determination, to gain audience with citizens all over the state and present them a message based on truth, and facts, mostly without the support or participation of elected representatives, who, even if they were sympathetic to the cause, fell back on the tired excuse that the issue was too complicated for the average citizen, somehow missing the point completely. The fact that ACCR has thousands of members contributing to its efforts, and was able to present state representatives a petition with over 60,000 signatures last spring calling for a bill which would have put the question of whether or not a constitutional convention should be convened,[*] seems to speak otherwise. "Indeed," Thomson wrote, "this growing bipartisan movement belied the scoffing of some legislators and special interests that no one cared about a new constitution."[100] The former, overcoming distrust, is an altogether different, and in many ways much more daunting, task. Once forfeited, trust can probably never really be completely regained, and any inroads achieved along those lines

---

[*] The bill was defeated, not democratically, but by procedural chicanery. Quite probably, it's best said in Latin: *quod erat demonstrandum.*

are equal proportions of trust and faith, at best, which makes the task evermore difficult because faith relies on overarching, ultimate instincts and beliefs that are all too easily assailed.

Such, I'm afraid, is the case with Annie Jean's children. As much as they may want to believe that there is such a thing, ultimately, as justice, in their day-to-day lives they don't see it, haven't experienced it. They lost their trust in that system a long time ago, and have placed their faith in us to rectify the situation as best as can be. So far, frankly, they haven't received much return on that investment.

Still, there's hope, hope for constitutional reform, anyway. The movement is growing. College students across the state are mobilizing, educating themselves to the issue, raising their voices. With a little luck, a lot of work, and some genuine legislative leadership, a constitutional referendum could be on the ballot as early as November 2007, about the time this book is scheduled for publication. Far too long in the making, obviously, but that is the stuff of hope—not assurance, or promise, but a simple chance, the final refusal to give up on the possibility of a brighter future.

I wish I could say the same for Ralph, Joyce, Brenda, Linda, Fred, Theresa, and Lonnie. The last time we met with Joyce, she had contacted all of the others still living in the area and invited them to the meeting. None of them showed. Disinterested? I don't think so. We were only in the midst of our investigation at the time, and had only gone, thinking about it in retrospect, as a show of, well, faith, to demonstrate to them that we were still working on the case. After forty years, it's easy to see how they'd be more than a little tired of shows of any kind. They, quite rightly, wanted answers. The next time we go back, it won't be without answers, whatever they turn out to be.

QED

ALMOST EXACTLY THREE months after we met with District Attorney Billy, I heard back from him. In an email message he said, "I checked with Ken Taylor and it does not seem to be any information that would be helpful. I did however, check the statute and found that Grand Jury proceedings are to remain secret pursuant to Code of Alabama Section 12-16-214, so regardless of the content of the file, I would be precluded from providing it. I do, however, wish you well with your book."

When I wrote him back I didn't say what I wanted to say. I reminded him that we were familiar with the code, that Taylor had in fact read it to me over the phone, and that it includes the pertinent provision – "12-16-221" I corrected, or redirected him – in the interests of justice, for the DA to authorize release of the proceedings, which was why we'd contacted him in the first place. I even told him about the responses I'd gotten from pathologists and the FBI expert. "It's pretty clear," I concluded, "that justice was not served, but then, the Barnes children have known that all along."

"That's the end of Steve Billy," Suzanne said.

"Because of what I wrote?"

"Because he's not going to do anything."

"I wanted to say I thought it both disingenuous and symptomatic that he'd take that stance after we'd explained the whole situation and our reasons for meeting with him."

She just smiled.

"Now what?" I asked.

"We find that nurse. Or we find another judge."

"There's got to be someone out there," I reasoned.

Somewhere, there's a retired nurse who reputedly knows what happened that Saturday morning in September of 1966. We talked to Kathy Hill, a classmate of Suzanne's, whose mother was the director of nursing at the time and had been interviewed by investigators. Kathy couldn't remember much about the case, though she did give us the name of a nurse that would have been working at the hospital back then. When I reached her, at a nursing home in Brewton, she confessed to not remembering much of anything about the case, nor the names of any nurses who would have been working in the ER that night. She did suggest I call another nurse, a private nurse, who might be able to help. That phone call was both disappointing and surprising. Disappointing because she, too, couldn't dredge up any names of the nursing staff from forty years ago. She did say, though, more than once, "I thought she," meaning Annie Jean, "was dead when they found her at the cabin?" This, from a woman near enough to some of the principals involved that her knowledge had to be considered the next best thing to first-hand. Not that it really mattered, relative to the task at hand. But it was indeed curious to have come back around that loop again.

At the time, I felt pretty certain, considering everything we've found out, that if Annie Jean wasn't dead when she was found, she was supposed to have been.

And somewhere, I'm just as certain, there's a judge who will recognize that, will see in it the travesty of justice, and will want to rectify the matter. That's the hope, anyway. Practically speaking, the historical record of such hopes is mixed, at best.

While Governor O'Neal may have been the first major political voice condemning the 1901 constitution, other voices, more aggrieved voices, voices of the document's immediate victims, were raised even before ratification. "Black opponents of the new constitution had promised that legal challengers would emerge," the Mobile Register reported in its prize-winning series, "Century of Shame."[101] Jackson W. Giles was one of those challengers. Four months after Governor William Jelks certified the constitution on November 21, 1901, Giles—despite meeting all of the other requirements: he was a federal postal employee, was educated, owned his own home, had even paid the poll tax—was denied registration by three white registrars in Montgomery because he was black. Giles organized the Colored Man's Suffrage Association and became the plaintiff in a series of lawsuits later known as the "Alabama Cases." The first step was in the court of Judge A. D. Sayre. "Predictably, Mr. Sayre had no sympathy. The judge was the epitome of the Black Belt aristocrat, as his son-in-law, novelist F. Scott Fitzgerald, later wrote."[102]

Appeals "took Mr. Giles all the way to the U.S. Supreme Court, where his counsel, Wilford H. Smith, became the first black lawyer to argue a case before the justices. Mr. Smith informed them that Montgomery Count registrars had refused to enroll more than 5,000 black voters solely because of their race, in violation of the 14th and 15th Amendments of the U.S. Constitution." Somehow, those judges didn't accept the premise that the issue was within their purview, rejected Smith's plea, and "declined to act on what Chief Justice Oliver Wendell Holmes Jr. dismissed as a political question."[103] Still, we hoped.

We hoped that both a DA and a district judge we were acquainted with in other parts of the state might be able to help somehow, at least direct us to someone who could help, but neither of those panned out, for reasons that didn't have anything to do with the case. We had access to other retired law enforcement officials and for a while it looked like they might take up the quest, but they suddenly became adamantly disinterested, strangely. Finally, we hoped that a nephew of the head nurse that night back in '66 might be able to come up with some names of other nurses. He never did.

Having exhausted all other possibilities, and maybe even feeling a little like Mr. Giles, who disappeared from the official record in 1904, I decided to call Scotty Byrne.

"Tell him I said hello," Gene said when he learned of the decision. "Tell him he owes me one," for the quail hunting trip to Georgia Gene had arranged years and years ago.

"Did he bag any?" I asked.

"Oh, yeah. A bunch."

But I never got a chance to relay the message.

"Mr. Byrne," I said, introducing myself. "I'm writing a story about Brewton and wondered if you'd answer a few questions."

"Sure," he answered, affably enough. "How long are you going to be in the area?"

"I'm not actually in Brewton right now, but I'm not far away, in Fairhope. I was hoping we could set a time to meet some time this weekend."

"What kind of story?"

"It's a book, actually, about the Annie Jean Barnes case."

"Who?"

"Jean Barnes."

"Oh, I don't remember anything about that, don't even remember what year that was."

"1966. She was found beaten in Dr. Perry's cabin, died in the hospital shortly afterward."

"Yeah, I know that. But I don't have anything else to say about it. All those people are dead, Chief Holt, Glen Holt..."

"Your office investigated the case, right? But no one was ever charged."

"That's right."

"I was just wondering why,"

"Look, I'm eighty damn years old! I'm trying to get all that stuff out, don't want nothing to mess my mind up."

"Well..."

And then he hung up.

"Wow," I said, staring at the dead phone.

"What'd he say?" Suzanne asked. She'd been listening to my end of the exchange.

I told her, emphasizing the concluding barrage, about stuff "messing" his mind up.

"How nice," she said, flatly.

"What do you mean?"

"How fortunate for him, to have that prerogative," she explained. "It's what we're all trying to do, isn't it?"

"True."

Some time after that Suzanne told me of a conversation she'd had with a friend of hers, who said Scotty's comment about not wanting that "stuff" to mess up his mind, sounded just like James Ford Seale's initial statement when they approached him about the forty-year old murders of Charles Moore and Henry Dee. Seale was convicted of kidnapping and conspiracy in the case this past June.

"Interesting, don't you think?" she said.

"Yeah," I told her. "But you know what they said about that case? They said it never would have gone back to trial if it hadn't been a civil rights case."

"So?"

Murder Creek

"So, I keep thinking about a quote I saw of Jerry Mitchell's. You remember Jerry, at the Clarion-Ledger, guy that kept after Seale, and Cherry, de la Beckwith, and Killen. He said, 'this notion that all you have to do is make some obligatory call to the target doesn't know much about journalism in my book.'"[104]

"Stop it."

"Now what?" Suzanne asked when we met a few days later.

"Now we arrange to meet the kids, and George."

"What are you going to tell them?"

"What we know, what we found out, what we think."

"That enough?"

"No, of course not."

We knew all along it could come to this. We even convinced ourselves that the effort was worthy, in and of itself, that just asking the questions was worthy, despite all the assurances that "they" wouldn't talk. Because the denials and the refusals are answers, after all. Are they answers enough? No.

But this much is true, I think: this is the permanent indictment Suzanne spoke of in her introduction, of the system, the system that had failed Jean, or worse, was engineered not to provide the same kind of protection for an Annie Jean Barnes as it did for a George Perry. While we may never see a particular indictment handed down, this permanent indictment of all those who aided and abetted that failure, that system, will suffice, is my hope.

We'd gotten the phrase from Fernando Botero, the Columbian artist who'd shocked the art world with his series of paintings depicting the torture at Abu Ghraib prison. "Botero has taken his sharpest departure yet from his normally placid scenes of chubby people and other still life paintings and sculptures," Dan Molinski of the Associated Press wrote of the series. Botero told the AP he was compelled to graphically express his outrage at the abuse. "I, like everyone else, was shocked by the barbarity, especially because the United States is supposed to be this model of compassion," he said.[105]

Referencing the work of his favorite impressionist, Velasquez, Botero told Juan Forero of the New York Times he "once thought that art should be inoffensive, since 'it doesn't have the capacity to change anything.' But with time, and his growing outrage, Botero said he had become more cognizant that art could and should make a statement. He pointed to the most famous anti-war painting of the 20th century, Picasso's masterpiece that depicted the German bombing of Guernica, Spain. Had Picasso not produced 'Guernica,' Botero said, the town would have been another footnote in the Spanish Civil War."[106]

When asked during an NPR interview we heard not too long ago, whether he was concerned that the work would engender any kind of recrimination or condemnation from the U.S., Botero answered, in essence, "Good!" He said art sometimes can, sometimes ought to serve as a permanent indictment, explaining, "They can sweep away the case, suppress the story, and its truth, make it disappear from the headlines and the broadcasts, but they can't erase the art." To that, to Baldwin, Picasso, West, Harrington, Thomson, Flynt, Annie Jean, Ralph, Joyce, and all the others, I say, "Amen."

Murder Creek

Postscript

SITTING AT THE bar in Old Willie's, downtown Brewton, Alabama, waiting for a phone call from Joyce, I heard the sound of that permanent indictment: the penetrating blast of a train whistle, as another freighter approached the main intersection of town, echoing towards us long before the split where 29 turns east—for the Buddy Mitchell bridge over Murder Creek and into East Brewton—and 31 veers north, through Brewton, past the White Horse Inn, and, at one time, all the way to Chicago. The sound reverberated long after the train had rumbled past. It's a sound that constantly punctuates time and life in Brewton, or marks it, depending upon how accustomed you become to the routine.

I wondered how used to such a thing you could ever be, wondered, rather, if it wasn't something more like an uncomfortable truth that refused to go away, shrill yet inarticulate, reminder enough, often enough, of the flaws in the fabric, the secrets buried, the truth of Annie Jean's demise, the injustices of the 1901 constitution.

But trains have always been part of the tapestry of Brewton, that there might not even be a Brewton, Alabama—or at least it wouldn't have been called Brewton—if not for that first train depot so long ago, and its first agent, Edmund Troupe Brewton. Perhaps the flaws and the secrets have always been part of that same weave, as well, and it's merely a matter of how you look at it, what will be seen, and what will be tucked away, out of sight.

"What are you going to say?" Suzanne asked.

We were trying to arrange a group meeting, with Joyce and as many of her brothers and sisters as possible, George Jr., and anyone else we'd talked to over the last couple of years who might be interested. I thought of it as a mirror image of the library event back in 2003 that had started us on this path, and even considered taking out an ad in the Standard—as Suzanne had—urging attendees to "leave their dignity at home."

Normally I go into these kinds of things unscripted, give enough of an overview and rely on questions to fill up the allotted time. For this occasion, I would have a script—this manuscript, sitting on the podium. I'll have an overview, a summation, really, of our conclusions. But I'll also have my own questions, far too many of them, which have yet to be answered. Why did it take the Escambia County Sheriff's Department so long to get involved in the case, if they ever really got involved at all? Why was the ABI investigation limited to homicide? Why was their report dated September 16th? Why did Byrne and Henderson ask Shoffiett to do the autopsy? Why was there never any official medical opinion as to the cause of Annie Jean's death? What happened to her medical record? And on, and on...

"I'm going to tell them what we believe," I said. "That the system was manipulated—whether deliberately, or because of incompetence doesn't really matter—in a complete miscarriage of justice, to make sure no one was ever brought to trial for what happened to her, from the investigation to the autopsy to the Grand Jury, all of it was skewed to protect everyone but Annie Jean. The inescapable facts are that she was brutally beaten—probably worse—and left for dead. The undeniable truth is, just like Gardner said, there is 'much in this community that is undesirable.' They had a chance to correct that, but they didn't."

"Pretty strong stuff."

"Too much?"

"No, no."

"I'll tell you what's most disappointing," I said tiredly. "Billy. I really thought he was our guy, that he would be the one to stand up and say, The case of Annie Jean Barnes is just another example of who wins the battle between power and faith, and who loses.

That doesn't mean it isn't wrong. That doesn't mean it isn't outrageous. It is outrageous, I am outraged, as you should be outraged, that these men brought before you have the temerity and the gall to think they can control truth and justice only to benefit themselves, because it isn't just Annie Jean's, or her family's loss. We all lose. We lose our faith, and our community. And I do not think you want to continue to live in that kind of community. I know I don't, which is why, ladies and gentlemen, it will be up to you to finish this story, why you must, you must find the defendants guilty as charged."

"Find who guilty?" Suzanne asked. "They're all dead."

"The system," I told her. "The whole damn system, from the constitution clear on down to the sheriff's office. Because you know what, I bet there's a legal mind out there who would see this as a civil rights case. Question is," I said, as my phone rang and I reached to answer, "can we find that person?"

About the authors

Joe Formichella is a former Hackney Literary award winner and Pushcart nominee. He has published two other works of nonfiction, A Condition of Freedom and Staying Ahead of the Posse as well as four novels. His other books are available on Amazon.com

Suzanne Hudson's novel In The Dark of the Moon as well as In a Temple of Trees and her short story collections are available at all fine retailers.

The two live together on Waterhole Branch outside of Fairhope, Alabama

Murder Creek

Notes

---

¹ *Inside Alabama: A Personal History of my state*, Harvey Jackson, Fire Ant Books, 2004.

² *History of Escambia County Alabama*, Annie C. Waters, The Reprint Company: Spartanburg, South Carolina, 1993, p. 17.

³ Ibid, p. 18.

⁴ Some of the above is adapted from Albert James Pickett's *History of Alabama*, 1851.

⁵ *History of Escambia County*, p. 22.

⁶ Ibid, p. 15.

⁷ Ibid, p. 3.

⁸ *A Journey in the Seaboard Slave States; With Remarks on Their Economy*, Frederick Law Olmsted, Dix and Edwards: New York, 1856.

⁹ *Screwed: The Undeclared War Against the Middle Class – And What We Can Do About It*, Berrett-Koehler Publishers: San Francisco, 2006, p. 15.

¹⁰ "An Analysis of Some Reconstruction Attitudes," in *The Journal of Southern*

History, vol. 12, no. 4 (Nov., 1946) pp. 469-486.

[11] *Brewton Standard*, September 29, 1966, p. 1.

[12] *Birmingham News*, October 1, 1966, p. 1.

[13] Ibid.

[14] *Brewton Standard*, September 29. 1966.

[15] *Birmingham News*, November 14, 1966, p. 1.

[16] *Official Proceedings of the Constitutional Convention of the State of Alabama, May 21st, 1901, to September 3rd, 1901*, Wetumpka Printing Co.: Wetumpka, AL, 1940, day 2.

[17] J. Michael Allen III and Jamison W. Hinds, "Alabama Constitutional Reform."

[18] *Alabama in the Twentieth Century*, p. 4.

[19] Ibid.

[20] Ibid., p. 5.

[21] Ibid., pp 6-7.

[22] *Official Proceedings of the Constitutional Convention of the State of Alabama*

[23] From *Brown America, The story of a New Race*, by Edwin R. Embree, Viking

Press, 1931.

[24] *Alabama in the Twentieth Century*, pp. 7-8.

[25] Ibid., p. 8.

[26] Ibid., p. 9.

[27] *Official Proceedings of the Constitutional Convention of the State of Alabama*

[28] Ibid., pp 11-12.

[29] Ibid., p 13.

[30] Ibid., pp 14-15.

[31] Edwin Stickland and Gene Wortsman, Vulcan Press: Birmingham, 1955.

[32] Personal correspondence with Paul Bresnick.

[33] *The Other America: Poverty in the United States*, Touchstone: New York, 1977, p. 4.

[34] Ibid., p. 5: a dubious benefit of mass production he says makes the poor *more* invisible.

[35] Ibid. p. 6.

[36] Certified and released by F. Taylor Noggle Jr., Director of the Alabama Department of Forensic

Sciences, Legal Custodian of Records, and notarized by Sheila P. Anderson.

[37] *Handbook for Federal Grand Jurors*, published by the Administrative Office of the United States Courts.

[38] Ibid, p. 5.

[39] Ibid, p. 2.

[40] Ibid, p. 6, emphasis added.

[41] *Press Register*, July 29, 2006, p. 1.

[42] *Vanity Fair*, November, 2005, p. 182.

[43] *Other America*, p. 14.

[44] *To the Mountaintop*, p. 182.

[45] *Where We Stand: Voices of Southern Dissent*, NewSouth Books: Montgomery, 2004, p. 88.

[46] *Other America*, p. 202.

[47] Ibid. p. 204.

[48] *Arrogance of Power*

[49] *Where We Stand*, p. 161.

[50] Ibid. p. 163.

[51] *Other America*, p. 206.

[52] *Democracy Matters: Winning the Fight Against Imperialism*, Penguin Books: New York, 2004, p. 16.

[53] *Other America*, p. 216.

[54] Ibid. p. 221.

[55] *A Century of Controversy*, p. 142.

[56] *Federalist #78*, Alexander Hamilton, 1788.

[57] *A Century of Controversy*, p. 149.

[58] Ibid. p. 142.

[59] *Official Proceedings of the Constitutional Convention of the State of Alabama*

[60] *A Century of Controversy*, p. 141.

[61] *Democracy Matters*, p. 3.

[62] Ibid. p. 13.

[63] Ibid. p. 16.

[64] Ibid. p. 68.

[65] Ibid. p. 16.

[66] Ibid. p. 17.

[67] Ibid. p. 19.

[68] Ibid. p. 15.

[69] Ibid. p. 20.

[70] Ibid. p. 80.

[71] *The Fire Next Time*, Dell Publishing: New York, 1962, p. 123.

[72] *Democracy Matters*, p. 23.

[73] Ibid.

[74] *A Century of Controversy*, p. 3.

[75] "The Struggle in Alabama for Constitutional Reform," H. Bailey Thomson, p. 14.

[76] *Official Proceedings*, day 2.

[77] *A Century of Controversy*, p. 50.

[78] "The Struggle in Alabama for Constitutional Reform," H. Bailey Thomson, p. 10.

[79] *A Century of Controversy*, p. 48.

[80] As reported by Thomas Spencer for the *Birmingham News*

[81] Ibid.

[82] Ibid.

[83] Ibid.

[84] "Alabama Constitutional Reform," as appeared in the Symposium Issue of the *Alabama Law Review*.

[85] Ibid.

[86] "The Struggle in Alabama for Constitutional Reform," p. 12.

[87] Ibid. p. 13.

[88] *A Century of Controversy*, p. vii.

[89] "The Struggle in Alabama for Constitutional Reform," p. 13.

[90] Ibid.

[91] Ibid. p. 18.

[92] Ibid.

[93] *A Century of Controversy*, p. 57.

[94] Ibid. p. ix.

[95] "The Struggle in Alabama for Constitutional Reform," p. 23.

[96] *Mobile Register*, "Let Us Convene," in its series, "Century of Shame,"

October 21, 2000.

[97] "The Struggle in Alabama for Constitutional Reform," p. 29.

[98] "The Election's No. 1 Issue," op-ed, *Anniston Star*, October 19, 2006.

[99] *The Birmingham News*, October 6, 2006.

[100] "The Struggle in Alabama for Constitutional Reform," p. 29.

[101] First of the series, "When the lights dimmed," October 15, 2000.

[102] Ibid.

[103] Ibid.

[104] *Mother Jones* interview by Joe Treen, January 24, 2007.

[105] The *Associated Press*, April 12, 2005.

[106] The *New York Times*, May 8, 2005.

www.ingramcontent.com/pod-product-compliance
Lightning Source LLC
Chambersburg PA
CBHW020900180526
45163CB00007B/2575